MIRROR ON THE WALL: WOULD MY DRESS CAUSE MY BROTHER TO FALL?

A Practical Guide To Sending The Right Message

By

Shirley R. Hawkins
Shirley R. Hawkins Ministries

Unless otherwise indicated, all scripture quotations are taken from the King James Version.

Copyright © 2012 by Shirley R. Hawkins
All rights reserved under US and International Copyright Law. Contents and/or cover may not be reproduced in whole or in part in any form without the expressed consent of the publisher.

ISBN: 978-1-6205-0266-2

Cover Design by Minister Lamont Coward
Layout Design by Overseer Iris Jones

Printed in the United States of America

Table of Contents

ACKNOWLEDGEMENTS ---------------------------------- i

FOREWORD by Elder Juliette Davis ------------------- iv

Chapters

1. Role Models In My Life
   [My He-roes And She-roes] ---------------------- 7

2. Knowing Your Body Types
   [What Is Your Body Type?] --------------------- 19

3. The Right Foundation --------------------------- 35

4. Will The Real Grandmothers Stand Up? ----- 49

5. Mirror On The Wall: Would My Dress
   Cause My Brother To Fall?
   [From A Male Perspective] ------------------- 59

6. The Proverbs 31 Woman ---------------------- 77

7. Are You Blending In Or Standing Out? ------ 85

In Memory of Pastor Valerie P. Taylor
November 29, 1957 - December 20, 2011

    Pastor Valerie was a woman of prophetic vision and insight for the will of God in the lives of individuals and the work of the ministry. The heart of her mission was to help young women. She held development classes for young women between the ages of 13-19 and taught them how to live as elegant, successful women of God. She held formal Young Women's Balls to honor the young women who successfully completed the development classes.

    Giving scholarships to these young women was part of her vision. She founded "Sisters of Life" Women's Ministry, where a difference is being made in the lives of women, both young and seasoned. Her legacy will continue to live through the Valerie P. Taylor Fund for Young Women.

    I acknowledge and dedicate this book to my dear friend, Pastor Valerie P. Taylor. This is also your book...I knew what you wanted to say!

ACKNOWLEDGEMENTS

I can truly say that God has been preparing me for this season in my life for quite a while. I never imagined that it would have been to this level; **writing my first book**. When you are sitting under an "Open Heaven," you always expect the unexpected. If God never does anything else for me, He has already done enough! This book could have never become a reality without the help of some very special guardian angels. I would like to thank the following persons:

Minister LaVonda Branch, my only daughter for your timely message to the wives. Your Women Conferences, "God's Trophy Wives" and "Reflecting His Image" have inspired women to be all that God has called them to be in Christ. Thank you for your love, patience and prayers. I appreciate the delicious home cooked meals and the many cups of tea you prepared for me during this process.

Kyia Hobson, my only granddaughter, a student at Liberty University in Lynchburg, Virginia. Thank you for your prayers and assisting in selecting the styles for the various body types. Your plays and conferences are truly making a difference in the lives of youth and young adults. I am so proud to be your grandmother!

My only sister, Sylvia Miller for giving me the space I needed to get to the End Zone. Our lives can now get back to some degree of normalcy. I appreciate your prayers, patience and understanding.

Overseer Iris Jones, my *one of a kind guardian angel.* You caught the vision with me from the very beginning and never wavered. You have taken multi-tasking to another level. I marvel at how you mastered the duties of proofreading, typesetting, editing and layout. Normally it takes several people to handle a completed manuscript for print, but you are a one (wo) man show. I am so grateful that God allowed our paths to cross. This was definitely a divine connection. Thanks for flowing in excellence from beginning to end.

Elder Juliette Davis, even though you were on overload and should have been resting, you took the time to write the foreword and the back cover. Thank you for assisting me in the delivery room. The baby has been delivered. Hallelujah!

Deacon Carrie Warrick and Naomi Brodie, thanks for always having my back. You have always been there for me; you have never said no. I appreciate our special friendship.

Minister Lamont Coward; for connecting with my Spirit and creating an awesome book cover. You gave me just the right blend. I appreciate you!

Dillard's Department Store: for providing the illustrations and detailed descriptions for the Foundation and Body Types chapters. I am deeply grateful to Karen Litton for providing me with additional information.

To the following manuscript contributors: Overseer Corey Todd, Mike Harris, Sheree Hilliard, Shamece Stewart, Minister Damilola Adeoye, and Overseer Patience Scott.

Sisters Betty Alexander, Conswayle Jefferson, Althea McKnight and Patricia Turner: my personal intercessors. I appreciate your prayers, text prayers, phone calls, and words of encouragement.

Bishop Daniel Robertson, Jr. and Co-Pastor Elena Robertson: for your willingness to bring the Word consistently, sharper than any two-edged sword. Bishop stated in one of his sermons that more would be required of us because of the kind of Word we receive on Wednesdays and **twice** on Sundays. I found that to be true. I appreciate the opportunity you have given me to speak to the Women of God. I don't take any of the assignments lightly.

My former Pastor, Dr. Lance Watson; thanks for grooming me for what I have been able to receive at Mt. Gilead. You taught me so much about leadership when you appointed me Director of the Capital Campaign ("Fulfilling the Promise"), to build the new facility. It was definitely a teachable moment, a challenge and a blessing!

FOREWORD

"Power is like being a lady... if you have to tell people you are, you aren't." – Margaret Thatcher

Margaret Thatcher was arguably one of the most influential women in the 20th Century. As Britain's first female prime minister, she earned the respect of the Parliament as well as heads of state. With a long list of accomplishments in her career, what I find most commendable is how she maintained her demeanor as a lady in a male dominated arena. Wearing her signature hat, pearls and modest make up, she fought many political battles without sacrificing the grace and distinction that separated her from the rest. This former prime minister knew something that we should all be reminded of today; being a lady is truly an inside job. Her quote says it best, "If you have to announce you're a lady – then it's likely that you are not one after all."

Sister Shirley Hawkins is the Margaret Thatcher in my life. She is a trailblazer who has many accomplishments to her credit, yet she is careful not to rest on her laurels and ignore the call to make a difference in this season. Now in the latter years of her life, God has preserved a wealth of wisdom and life experiences "for such a time as this." Written to reach the young as well as the young at heart; (***"Mirror On The Wall: Would My Dress Cause My Brother To Fall?"***) encourages a renewed level of consciousness about what it means to be a lady.

If there was ever a time when we needed a clarion call to restore the dignity and grace found in being "lady like," it is now. In this era of music videos, social networks, tweeting and texting, we have all but lost the value of self control and modesty. The advent of reality television seems to have created a generation of voyeurs (those who long to see it all) where more is better and nothing is left to the imagination. While I am grateful for the technology that allows us to reach the unreachable by simply hitting a switch, there is a price to be paid for the world of instant access. If it's true that what we see on television we will eventually see mirrored in our daily travels, than what does that tell us about the power of influence?

In a conscious attempt to tip the scales of influence in the other direction, Momma Shirley (as she is affectionately called), provides some practical information about the true anatomy of a lady. As with most of the critical lessons in our life, the journey to become a lady begins at home with role models who were instrumental in shaping her self image. Whether you are a parent, uncle, or grandparent, your contribution matters to those who would dare to pay attention. Some of the best lessons in life are learned by those with a "teachable spirit" – especially when you are surrounded by loved ones who are willing to tell you the truth.

And speaking of the truth, I encourage every woman to take your time reading the chapter subtitled; **"From A Male Perspective."** It's a reality check for those who have *"ears to hear and a heart to receive."* We are not always aware of the conflicting messages we send every day, but thank God this chapter helps us to see the error in our ways.

One of the most powerful messages found in (*"Mirror On The Wall: Would My Dress Cause My Brother To Fall?"*); is the chapter devoted to explaining what it means to represent God. If there are dress codes for the White House and even the court house, why isn't there one for God's house? Sister Hawkins challenges the reader to consider representing God as a lifestyle rather than something you do one day out of the week. As God begins to change your heart, you will become more conscious of how well you represent Him. When pleasing Him becomes your priority, adjusting your outward appearance will become your reasonable (minimum) service.

At the risk of being repetitive, being a lady is absolutely an inside job. His transformation power begins when we accept Jesus into our hearts and it is that acceptance that gives Him consent to begin renewing our minds. Our transformed minds will help us to overcome daily; to be in the world – but not of the world (Romans 12:1-2). (*"Mirror On The Wall: Would My Dress Cause My Brother To Fall?"*); is a reference tool written by a woman who learned a long time ago, that being a lady is not limited by your outward appearance, but it is the totality of your appearance and demeanor. Whether you are at church, in the workplace or at the gym, the lady in you will always be evident. This book is a timely word in due season. Read it and be blessed!

~Elder Juliette Davis~

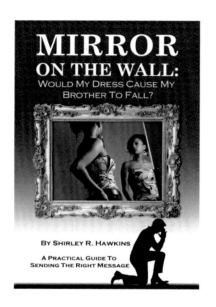

Let the reading begin!!

Chapter 1

ROLE MODELS IN MY LIFE
[My He-roes and She-roes]

I grew up in a family where appearance was very important. I was taught at an early age to look my very best. As a child, I marveled at how my parents, grandparents, uncles and aunts loved to dress. They all had their own individual style and I never had to look outside of the family for role models.

The women in the family always wore styles that complimented their individual figures. Their shoes and handbags always coordinated with their outfit. Of course, they were certain that their jewelry gave their attire that right touch. On Sundays, their beautiful hats and gloves always added the finishing touch to their outfits. When I was growing up, a lady never entered a worship service without her head covered. I can remember during my early adult years paying as much as $150.00 or more for a beautiful Mr. John hat. You would always know if a woman was wearing one because it stood out from any other hat in the room. I also purchased several of them for my grandmother.

My grandmother, Florence Ross who I affectionately called (Big Mama), was known for her beautiful hats at Good Shepherd Baptist Church in Richmond, Virginia. She was the mother of the church for many years. She would come home after Sunday service and share proudly how many compliments she received. Whenever I would go shopping for her, she would always say, "Baby, don't bring me anything old-fashioned. Be sure that you get something for me that you would like for yourself." She loved beautiful colors and stressed the importance of me not purchasing too many black or gray garments for her. She knew what season she was in and definitely stayed in her lane. She was very creative too. I can remember her sitting on the front porch making a skirt by hand. She often shared how she would take some of her old dresses and make dresses for my aunts to wear to school when they were little girls. They did not have a lot of money, but the creative juices flowed! There was a popular song out years ago that went something like this; "the whole world is a stage and everybody is playing a part." I can truly say that Big Mama played her part well as a wife, mother, grandmother and great-grandmother. She lived to be 93 years old, and until the very end, she was always conscious of her appearance. **That is the way to go!**

My grandfather, Jesse Ross, Sr. (Big Daddy) was a sharp dresser. Everything he wore matched from head to toe. He had a sports cap for every outfit. He never put it on straight, but wore it to the side. Years ago, men had to be certain that the shoes were so shiny that you could almost see your face in them. Even if he went to the grocery store, Big Daddy was going to look his best. The reason was simple; "you never knew who you might run into while you're shopping."

I can remember when young men had to wear belts to hold their pants up. A young man would have never displayed his underwear in front of a lady. He was to respect her at all times.

My mother, Dorothy Mae Ross was truly one of a kind. She loved to dress and had a figure that complimented any outfit. My mother always took great pride in her appearance. She loved her jewelry and was certain that whatever piece she wore accented her outfit to the fullest. In those days the women wore the stockings with the seam going up the back of the leg. Her seams were always straight. She wore the very same type of high heel shoes worn today! I always wondered how she walked in them. Actually, she strutted as though she was on a runway. My sister Sylvia and I would playfully try to imitate her, but we gave up. That was a one of a kind walk. On Sundays, other women would wear their hats in the center of their heads, but hers would tilt to the side. When she dressed up, I would always marvel how she could almost make an outfit talk. I know you have never heard it put quite this way, but in those days that was how I felt. She was a very confident person and early on she instilled the same in my sister and me.

My mother and father bought us some of the most beautiful clothes when we were growing up. They made sure that we were always neat and clean. During the summer when school was out, we would get up and put on our play clothes. In the evening we took a bath and put on clean clothes to go to the playground. We never kept on the same clothes all day. Oh, how times have changed!

My sister Sylvia and I were four years apart in age. Everyday our mother made sure that we were always dressed alike. Now this was okay when I was a little girl, but when I began to notice the boys, I did not want my little sister dressed like me. I had a difficult time trying to convince my mother that it wasn't that I didn't love my sister; I just did not want her looking like me. When I got my first job, I took my sister shopping and bought her lovely coats, dresses, etc. When she became a teenager, clothes were not as important to her as they were to me. My sister shared with me that she did not like dressing like me either; she never cared for all those frilly dresses. She commented, "I don't want to dress like you or be anything like you." She told me that she hated those outfits I bought her and only wore them occasionally when she was around me.

That was then, and this is now. We are closer than we have ever been. Her relationship with God has gone to another level and it has been a joy to watch her grow. You should see my sister's style of dress now. She still wears her **"Sunday Clothes"** on Sundays. I can truly say that she represents God well in her dress in all areas. I am so proud to call her my sister.

My father, Jesse Ross, Jr. wanted a son and since he never had one, he taught my sister and me all types of male sports. My Dad was a boxer in his early years. He often practiced hitting his boxing bag on a regular basis. Sometimes it appeared as though his huge muscles would pop through his shirts. Yes, you guessed it, my sister and I also had to practice hitting the bag as well. Can you imagine! Whenever he would take us to a baseball game, he would take the bows off the ends of our braids and tuck our braids under the baseball cap once he was out of the sight of my mother. He really wanted us to look like little boys. My mother did not find out about this until later in life.

My father also taught us how to pitch and catch a baseball in our back yard. Oh yes, and at Christmas time, we had our cowgirl outfits with the cap guns. I am grateful too that we still played our girlie games and had our beautiful dolls and dollhouses. Honestly, we were walking a thin line. I thank God for keeping my sister and me covered; guiding us and directing us in the way that we should go. Hallelujah! As the old timers used to say, "It could have been the other way." I am so grateful that we grew up and became young ladies.

My father was always neat in his appearance and always looked nice in his clothes. He was not into suits and dress hats as some of his brothers. He was mainly a sporty type of person. It was only in his later years that he had begun dropping his sporty look and had become more refined.

We did not have an abundance of money, but God supplied all of our needs and many of our wants. It still amazes me today how my mother and father were able to stretch that almighty dollar. I now realize that they used the wisdom that God had given them. My mother and father divorced when I was young. However, my mother continued to make sure that we had clothes and took pride in our appearance. I am sure this is why I love clothes today.

My mother's sister, Louise Grady (Aunt Louise) was a positive force in my life. She was a role model in every sense of the word. She had some of the most beautiful and intricate laced ruffled and frilly blouses I had ever seen. Aunt Louise could dress and always stood out in a crowd. My sister shared that she always wanted to dress like her when she grew up. Regardless of whether it was a dress, suit or skirt, Aunt Louise wore them well. Everything she wore we wished we had it for ourselves. Even at the age of 87, Aunt Louise lives in a retirement community and she is still very much conscious about her appearance. Her son, Keith and my sister Sylvia are her caregivers and they check on her daily and make sure she is properly dressed.

It is so interesting that if it is in your blood to look your very best, it never leaves you regardless of your condition or state of mind. She dressed Keith in the same fashion our parents dressed my sister Sylvia and me. Keith is heading into his seasoned years and still loves to hook up those outfits.

My Aunt Louise had been a nurse aid for many years. When she was in her fifties, she decided to go to the Medical College of Virginia to get her nursing degree. We all thought that it was inspiring to see her tackle Algebra and Geometry at her age. She hung in there and passed the courses. Words cannot describe how proud we all were of her. This was what you call determination. She was a nurse for many years and wore her uniforms proudly. We were always in awe at her crisp, well-ironed uniforms that conformed to her figure.

When you see a sharp-dressed person, female or male in the latter part of their senior years, they did not get that way over-night. Usually that individual has been that way their entire life. It gives me so much joy when I see a well-dressed older person. They appear to have so much pride. Check out their walk. It is as though they know they look good!

My mother's mother, Ellen Price (Grandma Price) also loved to dress. She took great pride in her appearance. Her colors were always coordinated. My aunts, Irene Ford (Aunt Irene) and Fannie Williams (Aunt Fannie) were two older aunts on my mother's side of the family who took dressing to another level. They wore the beautiful, expensive fur coats and exquisite shoes. They were in a league of their own. I did not spend as much time with them as I spent with my younger aunts; however, I admired and respected them. They were ladies who demanded respect and I learned so much by just observing and listening to them. My aunts were no-nonsense individuals from the heart.

My father had two sisters and four brothers. These aunts and uncles played a very important part in my development. They instilled so much into me as a child and young adult. When I was growing up, when your aunts and uncles reprimanded you, it was the same as if your parents were doing so. They believed in the concept that it takes a village to raise a child. There was no talking back and changing your facial expressions. If I had done either, I probably would not be walking on my own today. When I was growing up, respect for adults, neighbors and teachers was not an option.

My aunt, Dorothy Sydnor (Aunt Dots) is my mild-mannered aunt and my father's youngest sister. I can truly say she was definitely one of my role models growing up. When I was a teenager at Armstrong High School, she was working there. I always knew that if I ran short of money for lunch, I could always count on her. She never told me no when I asked for it. I made a point of paying her back on the date that I promised. If I did not, she would remind me in such a meek manner. She was teaching me the importance of being a person of my word.

My Aunt Dots also made sure that when I was a teenager I had a safe place to entertain my friends. If we wanted to have a party or get-together, she made her family room available to us and it kept us from getting in trouble. Of course, they did an excellent job of chaperoning so that no one got out of hand. We also had many cookouts in her back yard as well. There was never any alcohol, smoking or drugs, just clean fun!

When I decided to make my own clothes, she taught me how to read the patterns and many of the basics starting out. She could make suits and even though I never got to her level, I would take any problems to her and she would gladly put me on the right track. I remember Aunt Dots assisting me in making an outfit for Easter. I was so proud of that outfit. I think she was even prouder than I was. I had a Shirley Hawkins' original and I did not have to worry about anyone else with my suit. After that, I was well on my way to making many garments for myself. It has been years since I have made a garment, but you never know; the creative juices may start flowing again in my seasoned years.

During her younger years, Aunt Dots had a very nice figure. She loved her clothes and hats and did an excellent job with her color schemes. Presently, at the age of 86, she is still coordinating those colors and outfits. She was always imparting wisdom into me, as did all of my aunts and uncles. She is currently living in a senior community and is enjoying life. Her mind is very sharp and she can still remember ages and dates as she did decades ago.

My aunt, Margaret Thompson who I call (Sister), was another one of my role models as a young girl. She is my father's oldest sister and has always been outspoken. You never had to wonder what was on her mind. However, she could put together an outfit from head to toe. I lived with my grandparents and my Uncle Albert from the age of 13 until I was 21. We were stretching the dollar and Sister would take her skirts and cut them down to fit me. I was so proud of those skirts because they did not look homemade and I received many compliments. In addition, no one else had a skirt like mine.

I ironed for Sister weekly and she would give me a certain amount of money for doing so. This enabled me to purchase my fabric and patterns to make my outfits. She taught me a lot about mixing and matching; although the young people call it coordinating. This taught me to put special emphasis on the importance of being an individualist, having a mind of my own, and creating my own style. As I became a teenager, I never wanted to dress like everyone else.

Sister at age 87 continued to dress until the very end. She went home to be with the Lord one day before this book went to print. While she will not have the opportunity to see the book in its finality; I was able to use some of the information she wanted me to include.

Every one of my aunts and uncles always shared the importance of dressing like a lady or as we would say today, in modesty. We could not wear anything that was too tight or too short.

My uncle, Albert Ross (Uncle Albert) was definitely a positive force in my life. He was going to re-enlist into the Army when he realized that my mother and father were having marital problems. He decided to stay at home and help raise me. He had no idea that at the age of 13, I would come to live with him and my grandparents. What would the world be today if there were more uncles like him? He would pay us (his nieces and nephews) a certain amount of money for every A and B we got on our report cards.

Uncle Albert taught me the importance of not being ashamed because I was the tallest girl in my class. One day I was complaining to him about my height and he asked me; "Miss Ann, would you rather be a midget or the height that you are?" I never complained about my height again. He began to teach me how to walk with a book on my head. The object was to keep it from falling off. I had to walk with my back straight and my head high. What would my posture be today as a seasoned citizen if he had not worked with me in this area? He insisted that I always sat with my feet flat on the floor and my back to the chair. He was mainly reinforcing what my mother and father had started.

He told me repeatedly that I must first have respect for myself in order for others to respect me. He always placed special emphasis on the importance of my good name. Uncle Albert would tell me repeatedly that if I did something to ruin it, it was going to be hard to get it back. He taught me what it was to flow in excellence at an early age in every area of my life. I could not turn in a report with any erasures or incorrect grammar. He would check each page and made me do it over again if it did not please him.

He too loved his clothes and took great pride in his appearance. He could hook up a suit, tie and pocket square. Of course, he had to have the matching hat. He did not have the money to purchase those suits in the magazines; however, he was a great imitator. He subscribed to Ebony and Jet magazines for me so I could see the latest styles for females. He always told me to make sure that the men I date are always neat in appearance so that we would complement each other. He definitely kept me well informed. I would often ask his opinion on how I looked in an outfit. I knew he was going to give me his honest opinion. If he told me that it was inappropriate, I immediately took it off. Whenever he complimented me on my attire, it would make my day. He often told me how proud he was of me.

I always enjoyed studying our Sunday school lessons together. He encouraged me to study God's Word on a regular basis. Uncle Albert taught me so many life lessons and imparted so much wisdom that it would take another book to share it all. Uncle Albert passed away last year, but his legacy will live on forever.

My uncle, Raymond Ross (Uncle Raymond) was another positive role model. He was the head tailor at Thalhimers on Broad Street for many years. When they went out of business; he opened his own shop, North Central Tailors on Chamberlayne Avenue in Richmond, Virginia. His clientele included doctors, lawyers, senators, governors and people from all walks of life. They followed him to his new location mainly because of the quality of his work. He was a professional in every sense of the word.

He dressed Monday through Friday just as he did on Sundays. The suit, shirt, tie, pocket square and shoes were all matching. His attire would not be complete without his hat to accent the entire outfit. Uncle Raymond was a sharp dresser.

There were two other uncles in my life as well. My uncle, James Ross (Uncle James) worked at the post office for many years. When I was little, I used to call him my rich uncle. He was one sharp dresser. He wore expensive suits and shoes and drove such nice cars. I thought my Uncle James had it going on! He always gave me words of encouragement from my childhood to my adulthood.

My uncle, Clarence Ross (Uncle Clarence) was not much into dressing as the others, but he was always neat and clean. He was truly one of a kind. I can say that there was never a dull moment when he was around. I remember him taking me for rides in his shiny cars. He would tell me that I had to put on my clean clothes if I was going to ride in his car.

It is so important that men step up to the plate and become fathers and uncles as they were years ago. Women must become role models to their daughters, granddaughters and nieces. **YOU MUST TAKE A STAND! IT IS TIME OUT FOR COMPROMISE!** You should want to live your life so others will be able to see the light that they have been in search of for such a long time.

There was no way I could have written this book without first explaining to you that it was by the Grace of God, and the wonderful role models He placed in my life that got me to where I am today. It was important to me to provide space in this book to acknowledge all of them.

I pray that this book will be able to take you from revelation to manifestation.

GET READY, GET READY, GET READY!

Chapter 2

KNOWING YOUR BODY TYPES
[What is your body type?]

Every woman must know her body type before she can make adjustments in her dress and move forward. This allows her to accentuate her best assets. God made each and every one of us different. He gave us the bodies He wanted us to have. Unfortunately, many women have no clue what to wear to compliment those figures. We will explore different categories so there will be no doubt in your mind what body type you are.

As women of God, we want to represent God in every area of our lives. This definitely pertains to the area of dress. Recently, I had the honor and privilege to speak at our Women of the Word (W.O.W.) fellowship at Mt. Gilead Full Gospel International Ministries in Richmond, Virginia; under the leadership of Bishop Daniel Robertson, Jr. and Co-Pastor Elena Robertson. My session was entitled; "Modesty is the best policy: Spirit/Soul/Body." After that session, many of the women shared with me that they were never taught many of the subjects we will be discussing in the upcoming chapters. I was able to hit some of the subjects briefly; however, I now have the opportunity to elaborate.

I want you to be able to walk into a room and the whole atmosphere changes because of your dress and the pure anointing on your life. I pray that there will be a renewal of the minds (Romans 12:2).

Knowing your basic body shape and understanding the types of clothes that will accentuate your good features means you will be able to dress in a way that really suits you and God. Today, there are many options from which to choose. You will be able to find something that will compliment your body shape, personality and life style.

So often, many women focus on specific areas such as the stomach, bottom, thighs, etc., which in many cases can cloud your judgment when it comes to looking at the total picture. To get a clear picture, look at yourself in the mirror in your underwear. It is always best to stand with your legs together and your arms a bit away from your sides.

Examine the area from under your arms; pass your bust and ribcage, over your waist and hips to the fullest part of your thighs. By focusing on emphasizing the positive and minimizing the negative, you can flatter any body type. The proper attire can draw attention away from any imperfection. Now look at the shapes in this book. Once you determine your exact body shape, you are well on your way.

Are you ready to learn more about your body type? The names of the various body types have changed in recent years and for the sake of time and space, I am going to use the following basic types:

1.) **Inverted Triangle/Apple Shape**
2.) **Triangle/Pear Shape**
3.) **Rectangle/Banana Body Shape**
4.) **Hourglass**

The Hourglass Shape is the ideal figure type. This is the type to keep in mind when considering clothing options. Try to create the illusion of an hourglass shape regardless of **whether you possess one or not**. If you are successful in doing this, you will succeed in emphasizing the areas you want to emphasize and de-emphasizing the others.

Some of the recommendations that you are about to read may change based on other features; such as your age, weight, face shape, neck length and figure flaws you may have. However, as women of God, you will have a guideline as to what works best for you. God did promise us that He would guide and direct us in the way that we should go!

Usually by focusing on small tips, every shopping trip will be an excellent opportunity to gain an item that will add to your wardrobe in a positive manner.

When shopping for your body type, remember that it is not about the trend. It may be in style at that particular moment, but you must be honest with yourself and the question should always be; "Is this going to compliment my figure?" No matter how easy it may be to fall into the trap of trend shopping, please resist. **I can testify that shopping for your body type will outweigh the costs in the end.**

STYLES TO ACCENTUATE THE
INVERTED TRIANGLE/APPLE BODY SHAPE

EXAMPLES: NAOMI CAMPBELL & DEMI MOORE

- ❖ Proportionally broad shoulders which are wider than your hips (so-called clothes hanger shoulders).
- ❖ Narrow hips.
- ❖ Sporty and athletic physique.
- ❖ Nice lean legs.
- ❖ Small average waistline and less defined.
- ❖ Large chest or bust for your frame.

Top-heavy women tend to fall into this category. In other words, you are heavy at the top and narrow at the bottom. This is the second best female shape (after the **Hourglass Figure**). It is critical for this body type to find balance by bringing volume and width around the hip area. This will help you achieve a balanced look. If this is accomplished, the waist will become the focus point in place of the chest or shoulders.

Fashion Tips for the Inverted Triangle/Apple Body Shape

- ❖ Look for items that have few details on top, allowing all the focus to be on the bottom half of your body. Design features at the bottom like a chain, ruffles, tiers, etc.; takes away the attention from the heavy bust and shoulder area creating an illusion of wider hips.

- ❖ Since this body type in many cases may need a different size for the top and bottom, consider separates.

- ❖ Consider flared pants & wide leg jeans which will help balance out the larger upper portion of the body.

- ❖ If you are petite, be certain to wear a tailored or fitted top with the flare/wide leg pants.

❖ Try wearing lighter colors on the bottom and darker colors on the top. In many cases, this will minimize the top half.

❖ <u>A-lines</u> work unusually well with this particular body type. Always use this rule when purchasing dresses, skirts and coats.

❖ Be certain to purchase tops, shirts and sweaters that nip at your waistline as well as flare out from your waist or bust. Belted cardigans and tunics fall in this category.

Inverted Triangle/Apple Body Shape should avoid the following:

❖ It is always best for this shape to stay away from stiff, bulky fabrics.

❖ Avoid big collars, high necklines and any style that will focus the attention to your shoulders.

❖ Beware of pencil skirts and tapered pants which have a tendency to accentuate the width of the upper body.

STYLES TO ACCENTUATE THE TRIANGLE/PEAR BODY SHAPE

EXAMPLE: CECE WINANS

- ❖ Hips and thighs are wider than your shoulders, bust and waist.
- ❖ Narrow shoulders.
- ❖ Extra weight is usually carried in the thigh area.
- ❖ Waist has a tendency to be small.

Women who are bottom heavy tend to fall into this category. Bottom-heavy shapes benefit greatly from styles that accentuate the top half of the body.

Always keep volume in mind where the shoulders are a concern when purchasing a dress for this body type. The goal is to bring the attention to the top portion of the body.

Fashion Tips for the Triangle/Pear Body Shape

- ❖ Consider wearing light colors on top and darker colors on the bottom. Darker colors will make you appear smaller.

- ❖ Since this body type needs a different size on the top than the bottom, separates are a **great choice**.

- ❖ Wrap dresses and tops with unique buttons or other ornaments that will take the attention away from the hips.

- ❖ Dresses with empire waistlines are usually roomier at the bottom and will not cling to the hips.

- ❖ Garments with embellishments near the collar and shoulder always works well.

- ❖ A large collar or lapel will draw the attention to your upper body.

- ❖ You may also want to consider tops with a round, wide or boat-neck.

- ❖ Wide and straight leg pants will help to create slenderizing lines on this body type.

- ❖ Slightly flared or A-line dresses, skirts and coats that cinch in at the waist and flow away from the body will minimize the hip area.

- ❖ Belts are always an excellent way of taking attention away from the hips. The key is to draw attention to your small waist.

Triangle/Pear Body Shape should avoid the following clothing:

- ❖ Coats that come above the hip; instead concentrate on the knee or hip-length styles.

- ❖ Pants and skirts with pleats; these will give additional bulges and bumps.

- ❖ Tapered skirts and pants; have a tendency to make your hips and thighs look larger.

- ❖ Baggy garments; these types of garments will only make you look larger.

STYLES TO ACCENTUATE THE RECTANGLE/BANANA BODY SHAPE

EXAMPLES: SARA JESSICA PARKER & KATE HUDSON

- ❖ Bust and shoulders are the same width as the hip-line.
- ❖ Waist falls in line with the shoulders and hips; little or no waist definition.
- ❖ Longer legs.
- ❖ There are no curves associated with this body type.
- ❖ May possess a small bust.

The female with this body type is straight up and down like a ruler. Due to the lack of curves, the rectangle in *some cases* has a boyish look. The positive thing on possessing a rectangular shape is that when weight gain and loss occurs, it is over the entire body. The goal to dressing right for this type is balance. This was the Twiggy look in the 60s. There are many fashionable pieces available today that will really help you create your own signature look.

Fashion Tips for the Rectangle/Banana Body Shape

- ❖ Create some curves by wearing belts to create a waistline.

- ❖ Shoulder pads will help emphasize the shoulders and work wonders for this body type. They can add some dimensions to the upper body frame. Be certain they are not too large or visible.

- ❖ Scoop and V-necklines will create volume near the chest allowing it to appear fuller.

- ❖ Embellished necklines can also work miracles and have the same effect as the necklines above.

- ❖ Do wear dresses that wrap or flow through the waistline. Empire waist skirts, pants and dresses work well.

❖ Wear skirts that will create curves in the hips. Pleats and ruffles are just two of the many that will give this effect.

❖ <u>Semi-fitted</u> clothes are this type's best friend.

❖ Gently flared, straight flat-fronted pants will help balance out your look.

Rectangle/Banana Body Shape should avoid the following:

❖ This body type should never wear baggy pants and tops unless it is around the house.

❖ Clingy and fitted clothes will not give you a balanced look.

❖ Low necklines are definitely a no-no.

❖ Narrow or pencil skirts are not your best friend.

❖ Vertical Stripes.

❖ Double-breasted coats or boxey jackets.

❖ Chunky wedge shoes.

STYLES TO ACCENTUATE THE HOURGLASS BODY SHAPE

EXAMPLES: MARILYN MONROE & HALLE BERRY

- ❖ An equally balanced upper and lower body (bust and shoulders are at the same width as the hips).
- ❖ **Well defined waistline.**
- ❖ Difference between the shoulder and/or hip measurement and the waist measurement is approximately ten inches.
- ❖ This figure resembles a coke bottle.
- ❖ Shapely legs.

Since this is the most popular and sought after body figure, I would like to share with you what women went through to acquire this figure. During the 1800s and Victorian era, fashionable women did literally whatever it took in order to achieve the hourglass figure and tiny waist that accompanied it. Foundation garments, corsets, breast-enhancing bras were extremely uncomfortable for the wearer. Researchers now reveal that some women probably suffered from a variety of serious health problems including the displacement of various organs caused by pressure from the corset. In addition, deformed ribs developed because the corset pulled the lower ribs to an unnatural position.

Girdles started to replace corsets in the 1930s. There were six million purchased in Britain in nine months. The girdles were far more comfortable than the corsets. You were still glad to get out of it at the end of the day.

Control top pantyhose are a type of nylon/ stockings that provides extra support to the buttocks and stomach area. They came into style in the mid 1960s at about the same time that many women stop wearing girdles. Some considered the girdles heavy and restrictive but many women still wear them today. With pantyhose, additional support garments are not necessary. You can keep these on all day with no problem. In addition, because of the cotton crotch, panties are optional. This is an excellent way of eliminating the panty-line. Women were equally excited when they decided to produce them in various colors. I will share more on the appropriate foundation in the next chapter.

An Hourglass body type can wear practically anything and look good. These bodies actually look like an hourglass and are considered the ideal body shape. Their friends usually envy them. Did you know that only 8.4% of women have the hourglass figure? When gaining weight, the fat usually stores evenly throughout the body. The shopping list for the hourglass body type is unlimited; however, there are still some great pointers to make your best assets realized.

Fashion Tips for your Hourglass Body Shape

- ❖ Slimming pencil/straight skirts work well. If you chose to wear A-lines, a lot of layering at the top of the body will balance out your look and make your outfit complete.

- ❖ Wear garments that draw attention to the **well-defined waist**. This will also show off the balanced chest and hips.

- ❖ Concentrate on fitted and semi-fitted clothes.

- ❖ Belts, ribbons, necklaces or built-in embellishment take your look to high drama while continuing to focus on the midsection. Belts are this body shape's best friend.

Hourglass Body Shapes should avoid the following:

- ❖ Very tapered pants.
- ❖ Avoid skirts with open pleats.
- ❖ Stay away from baggy styles (remember you have the perfect figure).

YOUR DIFFERENT BODY TYPES

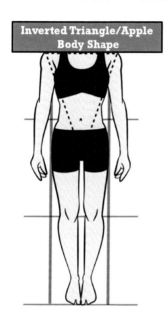
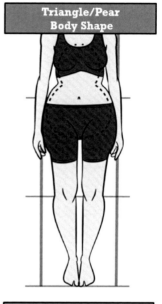
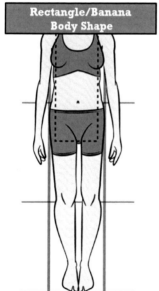
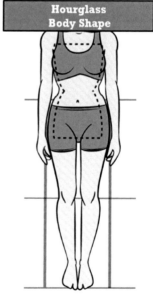

Chapter 3

THE RIGHT FOUNDATION

Ladies, the right foundation under your garment reveals a lot about you. My Spirit has grieved on numerous occasions when I see how Christian women are representing God with their dress attire. I cannot believe that women are walking down the church aisles with so much movement. As the old saying use to go; "there appears to be no shame in their game."

I can remember when a woman wore a girdle to keep down the movement in the buttock area. These girdles were not comfortable and you could not wait to get home to get out of them. We also wore the three-inch long-line bra to meet the top of the girdle. This was a necessity to be certain that your clothes fit properly. As time progressed, women got away from the girdles and began to wear the control top pantyhose. They gave you some control; however, they could not stand up against the control needed that the girdles offered.

Many women today are not wearing any type of control. Some of them are extremely over-weight. Spanx is used for control and to avoid the panty-line. A woman's undergarment wardrobe is not complete without some shape-wear. There are foundation garments for every figure, outfit and checkbook. I suggest that you wear shapers with your dress. This will prevent the bumps and bulges from showing underneath.

It is always good to have various types in your closet. Your attire will determine the type of shaper you should wear on a particular day. Always remember to use a light control garment when wearing a jogging suit, sports attire, etc. to church. For some reason, women just let it all hang loose because these are comfy clothes. That is true, but when we enter our places of worship, we don't want to be too loose. I notice that women wear these outfits to church for meetings, rehearsals and other activities during the week. The selection of athletic suits presently on the rack is simply awesome! I can remember when they only had one style. Your focus should always be on how much movement is taking place in the back. Remember, men are usually present as well as women. We must always have a mindset that I am going to check myself in the mirror thoroughly to be certain that my outfit is appropriate.

If you are in the Richmond, Virginia area, I highly recommend that you visit the manager and staff of the Lingerie Department at Dillard's in Short Pump Town Center. To schedule an appointment with them, you can call (804) 253-0182 Ext. 5200 or drop by while you are out shopping. They will give you that personal attention that is missing today. The manager and staff of the Lingerie Department make you feel like they are there just for you! Their knowledge of what works best for you is outstanding. You will find yourself looking at your body completely different. In other words, they know their products. How can you sell a product if you are not knowledgeable?

I was amazed at how much time they spent with me. It was not that attitude of; "will you please make up your mind, because I have other customers." Actually, this is how sales associates use to treat a customer; they made you feel special.

The Lingerie Department at Dillard's staff of associates is ready and willing to assist you. They are well trained, very friendly and knowledgeable. Occasionally, there are times when customers are eager to complain, but there should also be the same amount of eagerness to pay a compliment. On a scale from 1 to 10, this team is a number 10.

If you have family members, friends, co-workers or church members, tell them about the Lingerie Department at Dillard's Department Store. Many of them are in a position to purchase their garments there. If we flow in this manner, it will be a win-win situation for all involved.

I really don't want to leave anyone out of this equation. We are all at different financial levels; your budget may be tight, you may be jobless or you may be a single mother where every dollar has to count. You may have a child in college or a seasoned citizen stretching their social security check. In the back of your mind, you are trying to figure out how you can pay this amount for foundation when there are so many other places you could use this money. As mothers, we are always putting others before ourselves – this is that nurturing spirit in us. In this case, if we are going to represent God well in every area of our lives, we must add ourselves to our "Priority List." We must be mindful of what message we are sending out because of how we are dressed.

If Dillard's prices don't fit your current budget, there are other alternatives to getting the results needed. Target carries a Body Shaping line by Sarah Blakely, the creator of Spanx called; **"Assets."** These shapers are much less; however, there will not be an associate there to measure you properly and make the right recommendations.

Being an informed shopper is crucial if you are purchasing foundation for the first time. Even if it is not your first time, you need an expert's advice. I assure you that it can become confusing because there are so many different styles from which to choose. It is still a great idea to allow Dillard's staff to measure you. You can still purchase your items from Dillard's when your situation improves. In the meantime, you can be encouraged knowing that; "the best is yet to come."

On the next pages there are illustrations of various shape wear. They have a detailed description to assist you in making a wise choice.

Spanx "Skinny Britches" Hi-Waist Short Shaper
Item #03458107

Offering sheer shaping power in stunning shades and classic silhouettes, this hi-waist short shaper is the answer to your search for a slimming undergarment! It features:

- ultra-light sheer fabric construction
- extra-strong shaping capability, which firms from just below the bra through the tummy, hips, thighs and rear
- non-binding waistband and lay-flat fabric for comfort and smoothness
- laser-cut legs and edges to eliminate pinching, binding, and bulging
- cotton gusset

Of polyamide/Lycra® spandex. Imported.

Spanx "Slimplicity" Open-Bust Camisole
Item #03198664

This camisole provides all the benefits of a shaper, while letting you enjoy the comfort and fit of your own bra! Made of soft-to-the-touch fabric with single-layer compression to firm the tummy and love handles, it features a high back for slimming coverage and sheer edging for a simply elegant touch. Of nylon/spandex. (Bra not included.) Imported.

Spanx "Slimplicity" Lingerie-Strap Camisole
Item #03166158

This camisole is made of soft-to-the-touch fabric with single-layer compression to firm the tummy and love handles. It features adjustable lingerie straps for a perfect fit, darts that release compression to flatter the bust, plus sheer edging for a simply elegant touch. Of nylon/spandex. Imported.

Cabernet No-Panty-Line Brief
Item #01921738

Designed to give you a smooth, sleek look under your favorite fashions, this brief offers light control and no-ride leg grippers. Of nylon/spandex/cotton. Imported.

Cabernet Waist Cincher
Item #02115729

This waist cincher with secure hook-and-eye closure gives flattering shape to the midriff and tummy. Of nylon/spandex.

Only at Dillard's. Imported.

Spanx "Slim Cognito" Shape-Suit
Item #03090775

This seamless mid-thigh shaper looks like a bodysuit, but provides the all-in-one coverage of a slip! Perfect under skirts and shoulder-baring dresses, it features a removable underwire for lift and support, narrow adjustable straps for a comfortable fit, and a cotton double gusset for convenience. Of silky-smooth nylon/spandex/cotton that won't cling to clothes. Imported.

Spanx "Slim Cognito" Shape-Slip
Item #03189242

Ideal for every occasion when you want to wow, this shape-slip features graduated zoned compression that targets the tummy and back, a removable underwire for lift and support, and adjustable straps for a comfortable fit. Of nylon/spandex. Imported.

Spanx "Slimplicity" Half Slip
Item #03198709

This half slip shaper is made of soft-to-the-touch fabric with single-layer compression to firm the tummy, hips and thighs. It features a seam-free front, laser-cut edges and flat seams for a smooth look and feel that won't show through clothes. Of nylon/spandex. Imported.

Spanx "Higher Power" Brief Shaper
Item #03262330

This revolutionary design combines the comfort and breathability of a cotton panty with the figure-flattering benefits of shapewear. It features a brief panty with non-binding legbands to minimize the appearance of panty-lines and a high-waist hosiery top to shape the midriff and tummy. The soft waistband sits just under the bra line for a comfortable, secure fit. Hosiery top of nylon/Lycra® spandex. Imported.

Cabernet Tailored 34" Half Slip
Item #03678041

The perfect piece for layering under skirts and dresses, this Cabernet A-line half slip features a comfortable adjustable waist, side slit and lace detail at the hem.
- 34" long
- nylon
- machine washable

Cabernet Stretch Lace Full 26" Slip
Item #03678050

The perfect piece for layering under dresses, this Cabernet full slip features a flattering silhouette and lace detail at the hem and neckline.
- 26" long
- nylon
- machine washable

The Right Bra Fit

It is vitally important that your bra fit properly. Be certain that a trained individual measures you in order to get your proper fit. An ill-fitted bra takes away from your attire. The average active woman today demands that her foundation garments are comfortable, yet supportive and enhance her figure.

A correctly fitted bra should be comfortable, give good appearance and support delicate breast tissues. Many women unknowingly wear the wrong bra. When you select a bra for fit, you should always consider size, the style of the bra and the size of the cup. Always bear in mind that the *size of your bra has absolutely nothing to do with your bust size.* Any size bust can be found on any size figure. Bust sizes come in various sizes, but not all manufacturers make all sizes.

The style of the bra may have a great deal to do with whether you get a good fit. You may find that one style of bra in the same size, bust cup and brand will fit you better than another style of the same size, bust cup and brand. This is a very important point to keep in mind; some bras are designated as narrow, medium, and wide because of the division between the breasts. If your bra does not give a good division between breasts, but the size and cup seen to be right, try a different style.

Cleavage in the House of God

Now, let's talk about what is happening in our worship services. It appears as though many women are wearing the push-up bras like never before. This is because they want the cleavage to be noticed. Women of God, we must be cautious of the type of bras we are wearing when we come into our places of worship. If you are singing and you know you are going to be doing a lot of moving, you must wear a bra that will keep your breasts from bouncing up and down. In many cases when it is cold ladies, the nipples of our breasts have a tendency to get hard. If you are wearing a form-fitting top, your nipples are going to show through that top. This is certainly a distraction! You can now purchase at Dillard's and many of your major department stores, Comfy Cups which are great for wearing with your bra for soft shaping and **nipple concealment**. Another avenue you can take to keep your nipples from showing through your clothes is to purchase some Gel Petals. They look like small band-aids and fit directly over your nipples. Each petal gives you approximately twenty five wears.

If you are serving on a ministry where you are doing a lot of bending, consider not wearing a push-up bra. If you are sitting at a table where you are doing registration or something similar, again you must be mindful of the type of bra you are wearing. We must have reverence for the House of God. My pastor, Bishop Robertson often reminds his congregation that when our feet hit the pavement on the parking lot, we are on Holy Ground.

BEST PRACTICES FOR FITTING PROBLEMS

Correct Fitting bras will provide you with Lift, Comfort and Support while taking years and pounds off your figure.

Question: When should I get measured for a new bra?

Solution: We suggest you have your measurement checked every time you purchase new bras or at least once a year. Your "body shape" may have changed, even if your "body weight" has not, due to changes in your lifestyle and activity level.

Question: Do you bulge out of the top "and / or" the sides of your bra?

Solution: Breast tissue will bulge out of the top and / or sides of your bra for two reasons. First, you may be wearing a band or cup size that is too small. Second, the size could be correct, but not the style. In either case, consult a Fit Specialist to find a bra designed with a fuller shape and more support in the correct size.

Question: Does your bra ride up in the back?

Solution: Most likely, your bra is too big in the band and too shallow in the cup. You will need to consult a Fit Specialist to determine your correct size. A correctly fitting bra should stay even around your body all day long.

Question: Are your breasts two different sizes?

Solution: Most women do have one breast slightly larger than the other. Most times the difference is unnoticeable. There are times when the difference is significant. A stretch cup bra or a bra with a light lining will help to create a balanced look. The fuller breast always needs to be fit first.

Question: Are your bra straps digging into your shoulders?

Solution: You are depending on the straps of the bra for support rather than getting the support from the band. Try to snug up the band of the bra you are wearing. If that doesn't work, consult a Fit Specialist to determine the correct size to give you the proper support from the band of the bra and to relieve the pressure on your shoulders.

Question: Do your bra straps fall off your shoulders?

Solution: First, try tightening the straps of your current bra. If that doesn't help, it may be that your band is too loose and the cups too small. Consult a Fit Specialist to determine your correct size. Perhaps a bra with straps closer together in the back is the answer.

BRA IQ QUIZ

1. How many women are wearing the wrong size bra?
   a) 2 out of 10
   b) 8 out of 10
   c) 5 out of 10

2. Which of the following should you wash your intimates?
   a) Woolite
   b) Bleach
   c) A very mild soap (i.e.: Dreft, Forever New)

3. How often should you be measured for a bra?
   a) Once a year
   b) Once every 6 months
   c) With any weight changes 5-10 lbs

4. How long does a bra last?
   a) 4 to 6 months
   b) 2 to 3 years
   c) 1 to 2 years

5. Is it ok to put your bra(s) in the dryer?
   a) Yes, but on the lowest cycle
   b) No, always lay flat to dry

6. All bras fit the same no matter what style or brand?
   a) True
   b) False, all bras fit differently and should always be tried on.

7. Is it ok to wear the same bra a few days in a row?
   a) Yes, just to be sure to wash it once a week
   b) No, try to rotate wearing your bras, the oils in your body can break down the elastic more quickly when worn consecutively.

Answers: 1)b 2)c 3)c 4)a 5)b 6)b 7)b

Chapter 4

WILL THE REAL GRANDMOTHERS STAND UP?

The Bible says that you are wonderfully made (Psalm 139:14); we are children of God (John 1:12) and that your beauty is perfect (Ezekiel 16:14). We are made in God's image, in His excellence, exalted as daughters of the Most High God. Do you not know that your body is the temple of the Holy Spirit, who is in you, whom you have received from God? Therefore, honor God with your body. (I Corinthians 6:19-20)

Grandmothers, we are to honor God not only the way we talk and act, but also in our dress. Our dress should always show respect for ourselves as well as others. In fact, we have a biblical obligation to dress modestly and reflect holiness.

The world's attitude is; "if you have it, flaunt it," even if you are a grandmother. Leave as little to the imagination as possible.

In chapter one; "The Role Models in My Life," I shared the role each of them played in my development. It grieves my Spirit when I see the examples many of the grandmothers are to their granddaughters today. When I go to the shopping malls, church and other places, many of the grandmothers, mothers and granddaughters are wearing the same style. It has not always been this way. It actually looks ridiculous seeing a seasoned citizen still trying to dress like a teenager. Grandmothers, do you realize that you have had your day and it is time that you stay in your lane? In reality, you don't have the shape you had 20 or 30 years ago. There are many areas on our bodies that were once up that have fallen or drooped. This is all a part of life. There are fat rolls and bulges that refuse to go away. Many of you have done an excellent job exercising and maintaining your weight but we still must be honest with ourselves. ***This is a new season in your life, so why not just embrace it.***

There are beautiful styles today for the seasoned citizen. It is always exciting when you find what really works for you. This is why I dedicated an entire chapter to Body Types and what will complement your figure. I am convinced that many people don't know, and of course there are those who just don't care. They have decided that they are going to wear what they want to wear regardless of what others may say. I have heard many grandmothers say; "I am going to wear what I want to wear, they don't pay for my clothes; you only go this way but once." In other words, these women refuse to throw in the towel. Unfortunately, these are the same women you hear say; "their daughter/granddaughter is jealous because I have a better figure." Even if this is true, your daughter/granddaughter may have the age/shape to wear that outfit, and you don't!

I have lived long enough to know that if a person has a true on-going relationship with God; your attire is going to reflect it. Are you willing to be a **God Pleaser** instead of trying to satisfy man? I think we need to stay right here for a moment. I have been in church; yes, I did say church and witnessed grandmothers dressed inappropriately. They will wear the tight pants, skirts or jeans and have the audacity to pull a tight fitting top over it.

Helpful hints for wearing pants. These rules apply whether you are 16 or 66:

- ❖ Always remember when wearing pants that they should never be skin-tight, especially in the thigh or seat area. You should also be able to pull them away from the leg. This definitely applies in a church setting.

- ❖ "Panty-lines" should never be visible. To avoid this, try using control-top pantyhose or thigh shapers to create that smooth look.

- ❖ If the pants are tighter than they should be, a <u>loose fitting top</u> will hide the tight fit of the slacks/skirts in most cases.

If we were to be honest, many of our African American women are carrying a heavy load in the back. Therefore, before we leave our homes, we need to check our back and front views in a **full-length mirror**. This is especially important if we are going to worship the King of Kings and Lord of Lords. He deserves only our best!

I have seen many grandmothers that I knew were on fire for the Lord, but their dress attire was sending a completely different message. Many of our young people today don't have role models in the home; they are watching us. I don't want anyone to stumble because of my dress. You should dress appropriately not to cause your brother to stumble and fall.

I can remember when the mothers of the church would pull you aside if you were dressed in an inappropriate manner. They were the older women in the church that were always on the lookout. These women wore the nice suits, gloves and hats. In other words, they were in a position where they could correct you because of the way they dressed and carried themselves. If your dress was too short or too tight, they had the holy boldness to approach you. Has the "Spirit of Fear" crept in? I have heard several statements such as; "I am not going to approach those young people because they may curse me out. These young people are not going to listen to anyone."

Grandmothers, we must first show ourselves friendly before we can even think about approaching them. You cannot walk pass them Sunday after Sunday and never give them an encouraging word and then expect them to receive helpful criticism from you. I can truly say that I have been able to approach the young males, as well as females on anything that I did not think was appropriate. First, I always find a way to do it in love. Secondly, I give them praise on a regular basis if they participated during the service and did a fine job. If I hear something positive about any of them, I make it a priority to find them and give them words of encouragement. Acts of kindness like this will open up an awesome line of communication with the younger generation. It is important that we get out of our immediate group and spread some love! Come on, you can do it!

The older men mentored the young boys in church in the same manner that the women mentored the young girls when I was growing up. They would call you aside and would talk to your parents as well. You honored and respected them and when they gave you advice, you governed yourself accordingly. Some of them did not care if your feelings were hurt. They were going to make sure that you respected the House of God. Today, I appreciate those Sunday School teachers and leaders that made a difference in my life.

The designers today could care less how you look as a grandmother. Do you think they are concerned if you dress in a way that your granddaughter or daughter will respect you? Many of the designers in Paris and New York are atheists and know nothing at all regarding Christian values. They have one goal in mind and that is money, money, money. In fact, they are laughing all the way to the bank! Way in the back of your mind, you must realize that you should leave these styles to the younger generation. I have gone shopping and picked up an item that I simply adored; however, it was as though I heard a little voice say; "This is not for you." On numerous occasions I have wrestled with the thought of how I could make it look different, but in the end wisdom over-powered my everyday thinking.

Prayer is always the key in every situation. I am in the season in my life in which I totally depend on God for guidance and direction in every area of my life.

Grandmothers, can we talk about the cleavage issue? As a seasoned citizen, why are you exposing your breasts? It is now time to find tops and dresses that will cover those (little girls) up. I have been blown away to see seasoned citizens with tattoos on them also. As women age, the breasts have a tendency to become a little wrinkled and dried up. Do you really think they look inviting? If you are married, your husband should be the only one exposed to them. If you are single, you should have lived long enough to know, there is such a thing as self-respect.

Recently, I was at a shopping mall and observed three generations of a female family that had tattoos on their breasts. Look at what that grandmother is passing down. I strongly believe that many grandmothers decided to have this done after seeing their daughters and granddaughters with one. Someone shared with me that maybe the grandmothers had their breasts tattooed years ago. I don't accept that explanation. Years ago, it was unacceptable for a grandmother to have tattoos on the breasts. Today, in my opinion, many of the grandmothers are dressing worldly for attention. The pennant or necklace is falling into the center of the cleavage.

There are many beautiful, stylish tops and blouses available which can be worn and will make "grandmothers" look like the grandmothers that God has called them to be. You can be stylish without showing a lot of skin. I promise you that you will look much better. Why not start today by covering up more and exposing less.

I have also been in worship services and watched as a seasoned citizen bent over and the majority of her breasts were exposed. In order for this to have occurred, her top was too low from the onset.

Helpful hints for wearing blouses/shirts. These rules apply whether you are 16 or 66:

- ❖ The neckline should be no lower than 4 fingers below the collar bone.
- ❖ Blouses/Shirts should never be too tight in the bust area. Of course, stay away from very thin or sheer material.
- ❖ You never want to allow the shape of the bra to be seen in the back (if you can see it, it's too tight).
- ❖ Stay away from the spandex or very tight shirts; leave those to the younger generation.
- ❖ Try to avoid wearing tank tops in a church setting unless you cover it with a shirt, jacket or sweater. Be very mindful of sleeveless blouses. In many instances you can view the bra from the side which is definitely a no-no. You can always wear a tank top under a blouse that is too low-cut.

If you are sincere about making a change, God will show you how to dress your God-given body stylishly and modestly. You will be surprised at the positive comments you will receive. You may just happen to receive one from your granddaughter. This may encourage her to make adjustments in her appearance.

Presently, we need grandmothers that are willing to take a stand and allow their (**Big**) light to shine! Your granddaughters are watching the girls on BET and on prime-time television where they are almost half-naked. We are living in a society where children have a lot less boundaries. They see the same examples in the magazines for teens and adults. Cleavage exposed is the norm. As a grandmother, you still have a responsibility to help set the example and play a very important role in your granddaughter's life. As I indicated in a previous chapter; "it takes a village to raise a child."

I would have never allowed my daughter or granddaughter to be with me dressed inappropriately. When my daughter was a teenager; before she departed the house, I would always remind her to carry herself in a lady-like manner. Sometimes she would finish the sentence for me. She had the outfit in order but it was also important that her actions were going to represent God. If I had not been setting the example, it would have been difficult for me to lead her in the right direction. It is so interesting to see how she has raised her daughter in the same manner. I have heard her say on numerous occasions; "I don't care what others are doing, I am your mother." How many times did I use that phrase! Grandmothers must live beyond reproach.

In some circles, the terms <u>modesty</u> and <u>lady</u> appear to be old-fashioned or out-dated today. However, if you have not been sharing the meaning of these two terms with your granddaughter(s), please begin to do so now. There are many excellent books on both topics that you can purchase or borrow from the library.

Below are some definitions of a lady:
❖ A well-mannered and considerate young woman with high standards of proper behavior.
❖ A woman regarded as proper and virtuous.
❖ A well-behaved young girl.
❖ A woman who is refined, polite and well spoken.

The following definition of **"a lady with class"** sums it all up:

A lady of class is distinguished, holds herself in high standards and respects her body. She is someone who is capable of respecting herself and others. She cares about her reputation and treats others the way she wants to be treated. She has self-control in her manner and speech and is quick to hold her tongue. Whatever comes out of her mouth builds rather than tears down. She delights in everything lovely and feminine, but she is not afraid to speak out when necessary. She is compassionate and passionate, nurturing, unselfish and has poise in posture and character. She is firm in her beliefs and accomplishes anything she puts her mind to do. Her peers respect her for being truly female. She is charming, attractive and naturally funny, can laugh at herself, is not pretentious, is down to earth, does not act like someone she is not, has genuine love for others and is honest and not hypocritical. **A lady of class commands attention and respect wherever she goes, even without saying a word.**

If you have not been the grandmother that you know God has called you to be, now is the time to make those adjustments. There is nothing too hard for God; make the devil mad!

Chapter 5

MIRROR ON THE WALL: WOULD MY DRESS CAUSE MY BROTHER TO FALL?

[From A Male Perspective]

One of the greatest challenges facing many of our men today is lust. Many have shared how the short skirts, tight skirts, slit skirts, long skirts with slits to the knees, low-cut blouses, dresses, tight blouses, sheer blouses and form fitting dresses are all a distraction. Many feel that this is one more way for satan to take their minds off worshipping God during church service.

It is a known fact that tight clothing is as much a potential problem for men as skimpy clothing. One young man commented that tight skirts are very inviting and a potential for lust. He also stated that you don't need to see skin. In many cases, the women wearing these skirts and dresses provide all the curves. It is so important to remember that men are sight-oriented creatures.

One brother flatly stated; *"**Oh how I wish modest dressing would come back into style; that women would have more self respect in general and particularly more respect for the Lord's House.**"* This is a great concern for many men in the body of Christ of all ages.

It is our responsibility to assist our brothers, especially if you are a Woman of God. We must continue to look at ourselves in the mirror before leaving the house to be certain that our attire will not cause our brother to fall. Many are crying out for help. I have spoken to some who are struggling and are still involved in the club scene. In other words, they go to the club on Friday and Saturday nights and come to church on Sunday mornings. Many may have just left the club a few hours earlier before entering the House of God. They know that they cannot serve God and satan at the same time. They realize that they cannot continue to straddle the fence; they must make a choice.

What I hear repeatedly is; "when they come to church they see the same styles worn by the females there as that they see in the clubs." Many of them need to see a difference and presently the church females are blending in with those of the world. Those of you who are saved and filled with the Holy Spirit need to become bold and refuse to dress like the world.

I am convinced that Christianity is closer to the world in its lifestyle than any other time in recent history. It appears as though many Bible-preaching churches are moving away from a strong stand against sin and worldliness. They are embracing a peaceful compromise with the very world that mocks their message. It has become unpopular to teach and preach holy standards. The concept of personal holiness has completely disappeared from the pulpit and the pew.

Many pastors are afraid to address this subject of immodesty among women in the body of Christ for fear of losing members. I thank God for giving my pastor, Bishop Daniel Robertson, Jr. **"Holy Boldness."** He refuses to compromise as well as water down the Word. The Word comes forth from the pulpit, sharper than any two-edged sword (Hebrews 4:12). He challenges us on a consistent basis to live a life of holiness. He addresses from the pulpit the way women are to dress if they are coming to worship. Even though many have not grasped it as of this writing, I know Bishop will continue to address this issue until there is 100% renewing of the minds. Of course, he and his lovely wife Co-Pastor, Elena Robertson leads by example. They are role models for boys, girls, men and women who have never had role models in the home. If a female at Mt. Gilead is ever in doubt as to what to wear, all she has to do is look at our "Mighty Woman of God."

On different occasions, I have spoken with two male members of my church from two different generations on immodesty in the body of Christ, Overseer Corey Todd (Corey) and Brother Mike Harris (Mike). These men love the Lord and have a strong on-going relationship with Him. The part I admire about each of them is their "spirit of consistency." Corey and Mike are very faithful and rarely have I attended church without seeing both of them. These men are strong soldiers in God's army and a blessing to the "Body of Christ." Because of the age gap, they may not like the same type of music or wear the same type of clothing. However, they both agree that women of God should be more mindful of their dress attire when they come to worship.

Mike has been married to his lovely wife, Carolyn for 47 years. He plays the saxophone at our church and does an outstanding job. They both are true encouragers and have been so supportive to my daughter, granddaughter as well as myself. Mike has lived long enough to know that women did not come to worship service with certain body parts exposed as they do today.

I had a lengthy conversation with Mike regarding modesty and modesty in the church. He has taken this opportunity to share revelation knowledge with you.

Corey is 23 years old and is one of the Overseers of our Dance Ministry. He serves in various other capacities as well. Corey is a strong leader and is a role model to his younger brothers as well as the younger males at Mt. Gilead. He is also a role model to males his age and some who are older. I met Corey when I was waiting for my granddaughter to complete her Mime dance rehearsal at church. We began to talk as though we had known each other for years. I shared with him how my granddaughter was in the process of writing a play. He gave me his number and told me that if she needed help in any way to let him know. He was true to his word when my granddaughter's play premiered at the Henrico Theatre. Corey played one of the main characters. He also picked up cast members that needed a ride to rehearsals. He has also been supportive with all of her plays and conferences. Corey is a real man of God.

In the upcoming pages, Corey and Mike are about to share with you from a male's perspective. Now that I have given you a brief background on these two "Mighty Men of God," I want you to fasten your seat belts ladies because they are both coming to you **honest, direct** and **straightforward!**

Is God Concerned About Our Outward Appearance?
[From A Male Perspective]
Brother Mike Harris

In today's society, many believers, both male and female are convinced that God is only concerned about the inward man (1 Samuel 16:7 ...*for man looketh on the outward appearance, but the LORD looketh on the heart.*) Therefore, it is believed by many believers that we can do anything to our bodies, put anything on our bodies; but is it acceptable to God?

I APPEAL to you therefore, brethren, and beg of you in view of [all] the mercies of God, to make a decisive dedication of your bodies [presenting all your members and faculties] as a living sacrifice, holy (devoted, consecrated) and well pleasing to God, which is your reasonable (rational, intelligent) service and spiritual worship. (Romans 12:1 AMP)

I believe that there is enough evidence in the scriptures to establish the fact that this belief is merely one of the myths or false beliefs about God (Leviticus 19:28; Deuteronomy 22:5; 1 Corinthians 11:14-15; and 1 Timothy 2:9).

The Bible teaches us that God is excellent (Psalm 8:1); His way is perfect (Psalm 18:30); He's pure, lovely, of a good report, etc. (Philippians 4:8); He's righteous (Psalm 7:9); He's holy (Leviticus 20:7 & 26; Isaiah 6:3, 43:15; 1 Peter 1:15-16).

What is holiness? I am glad you asked. Holiness simply put, is living according to the Word of God. In years past and maybe still today, some religions required, especially the women, to wear certain attire such as long dresses or skirts (black or white in color) in order to be or look holy. I wonder what they would think today. The truth is, what you wear will not determine your holiness; however, your holiness will determine what you wear!

God created us (mankind) in an image and likeness of Himself (Genesis 1:26-27). Considering the above attributes of God, what kind of attributes should we display as sons and daughters of God? Should we not desire to live holy to the best of our ability?

I have been asked to give input (from a senior male perspective) concerning a matter in the "Body of Christ" in which the subject is too often looked over. This issue is the attire and appearance of many of our "Sisters-in-Christ."

What qualifies me to be able to give input concerning this issue? First of all, God has blessed me to reach the age of 70. I have been studying the Word of God for many years and I am still growing in the Word. I have many life experiences dealing with worldly and lustful situations resulting in numerous years of heartaches and disappointments!

I am a musician and have been involved in some form of music most of my life. Prior to accepting Jesus Christ as my personal Savior at the age of 45, I allowed the devil to use my musical gifts and talents for his glory.

I played music in a Rhythm and Blues (R&B) band for approximately 15 years; including performances at high school dances/proms, college activities (fraternity and sorority houses), dance halls, night clubs, stage shows, R&B shows, private parties, etc. During those years of performances, I've experienced a lot of lustful temptations and regretfully I yielded to many of those temptations. Although that happened years ago, I often deal with the consequences of those sinful deeds, even today!

There is a consequence for sin! One might ask, "What is sin?" All unrighteousness is sin (1 John 5:17). Sin is anything that's contrary to the "Word and Will of God." If righteousness (as described by many) is being in right-standing with God, then unrighteousness must be anything that is displeasing to God.

Can a person's appearance and attire be sinful? I believe it can if it causes that individual or others to go against the Will of God. Always remember, when we willfully sin, it is our choice; we can choose the sin, but we can't choose the consequences.

Now ladies, my dear "Sisters in Christ," there are some things that I believe the Lord God wants me to share; especially with you! He wants you to know and understand who you are to Him; who He created you to be.

Are you listening ladies? Please open your hearts and your spiritual ears – hear what the Lord is saying to you. Your Heavenly Father wants you to know that you are His daughters. He loves you tremendously. You are very, very, very special to Him. Do you not remember how He sent His only begotten son to die for you (John 3:16), in order to prove how much He loves you? Do you know how much He has invested in you and still sacrifice for you? Do you realize how pure and genuine His love is toward you?

Are you still listening ladies? Your Father wants you to always be aware that you are the righteousness of Him in Christ Jesus (2 Corinthians 5:21). He says that your body is His temple and He desires to dwell in you – if anyone defiles His temple (which you are), He will destroy them because His temple is holy (1 Corinthians 3:16-17, 6:19-20). You are the "apple of His eye."

Ladies, I pray that your heart and ears are still open because there's more to come. Please buckle your spiritual seat belts for the remainder of the trip!

Prior to delivering the rest of this message, I must tell you all that I love you and I care about my Sisters-in-Christ. People are often told and taught about God's amazing and unconditional love for us, which is great and very important to know. However, my question for you is, "How much do you love God?"

Ladies, do you love God enough to refrain from wearing those tight and provocative clothes that many of you often wear even to church, showing every "curve" in your body and sometimes enough "cleavage" to almost fill the offering bucket!

When I played music in the nightclubs and other venues, I often observed females wearing short, tight clothing and flaunting themselves in front of the band members and other men seeking attention. Sometimes they would even have the nerve to ask (if they saw you looking), "What are you looking at? They already knew that we were looking at what they were showing us.

This type of behavior is expected from non-believers and people in the world because they don't know Jesus. Should this behavior be common among believers and women of the Word? God forbid!

Some pastors, preachers and teachers often emphasize the fact that men are moved or motivated by what they see (that is the nature of men of all ages), especially when it pertains to the female. I believe that is what caused Adam to fall in the Garden of Eden.

Ladies, I hope you're not tired of listening, I'm almost finished. You have heard what God created you to be. Now let me share briefly what He did not create you to be. God did not create you to be a sex symbol, a prostitute nor a whoremonger! Therefore, be careful that you don't dress or appear as such.

God has too much invested in you. You belong to Him. You have been purchased with the precious blood of Jesus! Purpose in your heart to dress modestly, (1 Timothy 2:9-10) as a godly woman should dress.

You cannot afford to follow the fashions and fadds (FADD - fashioned after de devil) of this world! Fashion yourself after godly women who really love Jesus; in the Word and in good deeds!

Please remember ladies that you are chosen, you are royalty, you are a holy nation, a peculiar people (1 Peter 2:9). Did you notice that scripture said, *"peculiar"* (not weird)? The world system is weird – doing and saying anything for attention. You are Women of the Word (W.O.W.).

Always remember, whenever you leave your home you are on public display whether you realize it or not. As a believer you should set a standard for the world and set a standard in your home also. When it pertains to clothing, be aware that designers and manufacturers are there to make money.

Now, one last thing ladies and I'm finished. You can now unbuckle – this trip is completed. Did you see yourself in any of the aforementioned habits? Do you love God enough to repent and change? Do you love Him enough to allow Him to mature and develop you into that godly woman that He called you to be? He wants you to represent Him as a true woman of God, not compromising anything.

Beauty Through The Eyes Of A Man
[From A Male Perspective]
Overseer Corey Todd

There are three types of men; 1) the natural (worldly) man, 2) the carnal (half in the world and half in the church) man and the 3) spiritual (God-fearing) man. When it comes to the different types of men, are there any significant differences as to their desires, wants and needs when it pertains to women?

The misconception that most women have is the mindset of how a man feels and thinks. What the world fails to realize is, no matter the position or title, a man is still a man. This includes thugs, professors, bishops and janitors. It doesn't matter what kind of man you are; men are men. No, not all men are the same, but in fact all men face the same obstacles. A man is predominantly moved by what he **"sees"** versus what he hears. When you teach a man about an engine through a textbook, it is not nearly as effective in comparison to teaching him with an actual engine, showing and explaining the function of each part that makes up an engine. What is the point to all of this? It gives a woman a clear and ideal image behind the eyes of a man.

Since the days of Adam in the book of Genesis, God designed man to dominate the earth and everything within the earth. Adam, being the first man God created, established "MAN" as the head. In addition, God designed a woman to aid man and help with earthly tasks as well as spiritual tasks. In Genesis 2:21-25 paraphrasing, it talks about how God puts

Adam into a deep sleep and takes one of his ribs and creates a woman for him and presents her to him. From the beginning, God presented Eve to Adam as a gift, a blessing and a soul mate. The enemy sought to find a weakness in God's creation so he used deception. Once Eve fell into Satan's trap, she then went to Adam. God didn't punish Eve for their disobedience of eating from the "the tree of knowledge of good and evil," God came to Adam. He had already established him as the head; therefore, Adam is held accountable for Eve's actions.

What is one of the revelations of this story between Adam and Eve? What God meant for purity and righteousness, the enemy seeks to taint and mess up.

What about Sampson and Delilah or David and Bathsheba? There are stories in the Bible that show how satan uses a woman as a tactic to cause a man to stumble and fall.

The devil wants to use a man's desire to weaken him. It's been told that the enemy knows your weaknesses better then you do. It is true.

Compare events 2,000 years ago, all the way to events now in 2012; the enemy has been using the same tactic, just in different ways. Men are falling left and right; presidents, bishops, company executives and ordinary families. Affairs and divorces have been at an all-time high rate, but why? If God established the man to be the head, why is the man allowing his household to be destroyed? Mark 3:27 (NIV) states, "No one can enter a man's house without first tying him up. Then he can plunder the strong man's house." In Matthew 12:29, it says the same thing. So then why is the enemy after the MEN?

The devil knows if he can disrupt the foundation of the house, then the house and everything in it has to come down as well. What is the foundation? The foundation is the Man of the House.

"The thief cometh not, but for to steal, and to kill, and to destroy: I am come that they might have life, and that they might have it more abundantly." (John 10:10)

The enemy's main mission is to try to sabotage the purity of God's creation. He hates the mere fact that we are created in God's image and His likeness (Genesis 1:26).

There are many devices the enemy can use to hinder MAN. His favorite is the one area that is meant to be an asset and not a liability; **WOMEN**.

It is bad enough to see the world advertise women as sex objects. It is another thing when some women in the church dress in a way that is viewed as a sex object. Maybe that's a little extreme to say, but it's true.

Let me describe some of the things I have witnessed inside the church recently.

Scenario One: A woman wearing a skin tight dress up to her thighs and a short blouse that shows more cleavage than necessary; wearing no stockings, just high heels.

Scenario Two: A woman wearing leggings/jeggings and high heels with a shirt that is too short to cover her butt.

Scenario Three: Wearing "see through" clothes where your bra or undergarments are seen.

Scenario Four: Sitting in a chair with a short dress, with no lap cloth and your thighs are exposed.

Scenario Five: Wearing a short shirt with tight tight tight jeans that cuff your butt.

Scenario Six: Wearing blouses that you can only button up half way.

Scenario Seven: Wearing bareback clothes that show all your back skin.

Scenario Eight: Wearing blouses or shirts that "HUG" your chest so tight you are basically showing the outline of your chest.

Scenario Nine: Wearing "see through" shirts but wearing a different color bra underneath.

Scenario Ten: Wearing dresses and/or pants that are so tight that your panty-line can be seen outlined from the pants itself.

These are just some of the things I, as a man, as well as other men have witnessed inside the church. YES, it is a distraction, especially when you walk up to the altar to sow a seed or just walking around. A man can take a small intimate image and imagine the rest of a woman's body mentally. No, I'm not saying we do it all the time or even the majority of the time. We have that capability to do so whether other men admit to it or not. The attires I mentioned in the scenarios above are a distraction. All men see it, whether they are married or single. Men are men and I'm sure other women see it too. But now it's revealed.

If a man sees one area that attracts him, our flesh is going to want to see the whole body. That is where it is a fight to keep our head straight, our mind on Christ and off a woman's body; sometimes it is not easy. Remember, "Men are moved by what they see." If you are married or if you are dating someone, ask the male what was his first attraction to you? If he is honest with you, he will say it was a physical compliment versus a spiritual compliment, but it's natural.

Proverbs 18:22 says, **"Whoso findeth a wife findeth a good thing, and obtaineth favour of the LORD."** Men are going to look at a woman's outer image and be attracted to her. But ladies, don't give us the wrong image.

"Be careful, however, that the exercise of your freedom does not become a stumbling block to the weak." 1 Corinthians 8:9 (NIV)

> ***"But God does care when you use your freedom carelessly in a way that leads a Christian still vulnerable to those old associations to be thrown off track." 1 Corinthians 8:9 (Message)***

Ladies, I'm not telling you to dress like a nun. I am simply saying, "Check yourself before you leave the house." If you have questions concerning whether what you are wearing is appropriate, get an accountability partner. Most women don't know that what they are wearing is "toooooooo" attractive to a man's eye. That type of attraction should only be meant for her husband.

Unfortunately, you would expect the church environment to be a little more modest. Yes, the church is the people, but every person does not have the right intentions for coming to the Kingdom of God. Now that it has been revealed, God will hold you accountable for what you wear.

A man loves a beautiful woman. Look at Esther and even Ruth. They positioned themselves to be received by their Man of God. Not just any man, but they received the best. One thing a man loves is a woman of self-preservation, beauty and virtue; who values her body as a temple for God.

Proverbs 31 is the key scripture for an ideal woman. Not physically, but mentally and spiritually. A woman should never want to get to the point where she is considered a hindrance when God intended for her to be a blessing.

1 Peter 2:12 (NLT) says; ***"Be careful to live properly among your unbelieving neighbors. Then***

even if they accuse you of doing wrong, they will see your honorable behavior, and they will give honor to God when he judges the world."

1 Timothy 2:9 (NLT) says; *"And I want women to be modest in their appearance. They should wear decent and appropriate clothing and not draw attention to themselves by the way they fix their hair or by wearing gold or pearls or expensive clothes."*

1 Peter 3:3-4 (NIV) says; *"Your beauty should not come from outward adornment, such as braided hair and the wearing of gold jewelry and fine clothes. Instead, it should be that of your inner self, the unfading beauty of a gentle and quiet spirit, which is of great worth in God's sight."*

Some women feel because of their past childhood experiences, adult disappointments with men or low self-esteem issues, they need to compromise and/or go overboard in their attire. What she fails to realize is that she is doing more harm to her image and to society.

To a man, image is part of the qualifications to a virtuous woman. Some more than others, but all regard it as a common factor. Men take note of a woman who fits their qualification and those they need to stay away from. Image is very important.

This chapter is meant for those women who desire to be a true, pure hearted, woman of God. Ask God to reveal areas about yourself that you need help, whether it's your attitude, image, discipline, etc. You know you better than any other human. But who knows you better than the Creator himself? The choice is yours. God is going to hold each of us accountable for the decisions we make. God sees our heart and knows our motives for everything and anything we do.

You are beautiful. No woman is ugly because God did not make you that way. He said in Genesis 1:31 (AMP), ***"And God saw everything that He had made, and behold, it was very good (suitable, pleasant) and He approved it completely...,"*** that includes you. A man can tell when a woman is confident about her image simply by the way she dresses and carries herself in public. The enemy has convinced women that dressing exotic is the new fashion statement. In reality it has forced men, not in God's Will; to degrade them, treat them as objects instead of the Queens they are. It's time to change the cycle of imagery, both spiritually and physically. So, will the real virtuous Women of God stand up for the present and future generations to come? They will be a reflection of the legacy you leave behind. You can make a difference in a young woman's life, but it starts with you. Every Woman of God is predestined to receive her Boaz. What steps are you taking to qualify to be found?

Ladies, I remind you again, I'm not telling you to dress like a nun or even change your style. In all regards I am simply saying, "Check yourself before you leave. Make sure your attire is not too tight, short or revealing." The Bible tells us that, "Ye shall know the truth and the truth shall make you free." And with the same truth, teach other women. It is ok to be modest and beautiful. A Man of God loves a woman with that mindset.

Chapter 6

THE PROVERBS 31 WOMAN

The Proverbs 31 woman has been described as the ideal woman. If you are not careful you may find yourself asking; "Can I do all of this and remain in my right mind?" If you look very closely at verses 10-31, she almost appears to be a superwoman in today's society. Each verse describes distinctly what she does for her community and family. She has many talents; in fact, she was a manager, mother, merchant and wife. In addition, she was smart and industrious. She had very little time for herself and did all of this with very little to no sleep.

Ladies, before you start comparing yourself to this woman, we need to study Proverbs 31 in depth so that we can understand what God was intending with this instruction. Proverbs 31 is a summary of an entire woman's life. In other words, this woman did not achieve all of this in one day or one year. Today's superwoman wears many hats and is an expert when it comes to multi-tasking. In many cases, it has become a way of life and it has not really registered that you are already that Proverbs 31 woman.

It is important to keep in the forefront of your mind that if you are a woman after God's own heart, this will assist you greatly in becoming that Proverbs 31 woman. In fact, the two go hand in hand. As you go deep into this study, I promise that you will discover that it was, in other words; her **"heart."** We see her as thrifty, wise, helpful, good, reverent, diligent and energetic.

So often we look at Proverbs 31 for married women; however, it can be helpful for single women during their preparation time. If you are single, please read this excerpt from Bishop T. D. Jakes' "Woman Thou Art Loosed!" Bible. As single women, you have more time to prepare your attire for worship service than a woman married with two children. You have time to check your front, back view and make sure you have on the right foundation. While you are getting dressed, look at the mirror on the wall; "Would your dress cause your brother to fall?" And then ask God, "Am I representing you?"

God's Hand Maidens, (Joel 2:29)

Some of you don't understand the benefits of being single. In reality, while you're not married, you really ought to be involved with God. Single women often forget some very important advantages they have. At five o'clock in the morning, you can lie in bed and pray in the spirit until seven-thirty. You can lie prostrate on the floor and worship the Lord without having to answer to anyone. This time in your life is for you to charge up the battery cells. It's time to pamper - time to take luxurious baths in milk and honey. You can lie there in the bath, praising and worshiping the Lord for as long as you want.

Before you ask the Lord for another man, take care of Him. If you are not ministering to His needs, and yet you are always before Him asking Him to send you one of His princes to minister to, your prayers are not being heard because you are not being faithful to Him. When you become faithful in your singleness, then you will be better prepared to be faithful with a husband.

If you disregard the perfect husband, Jesus, you will certainly disregard the rest of us. The Lord wants you to come home at the end of a day and say, "Lord, I went through so much today. I am so glad You're here. I just couldn't wait to get alone and worship You and praise You and magnify You. Tonight is our night. I'm not so busy that I don't have time for You." If you don't have time for God, you don't have time for a husband.

There is nothing wrong with wanting to be married. Simply take care of the Lord while you're waiting. Minister to Him. Let Him heal you and loose you, and worship Him. Single women ought to be the most consecrated women in the church. You are the ones whose shadows ought to fall on people and they be healed. You are in a position of posture and prayer. The Lord has become your necessary food. While some married women are dependent on their husbands, single women learn to be dependent on the Lord. God told Joel, "...and on My maidservants I will pour out My Spirit" (Joel 2:29). There is a special relationship between God and the single believer. God has a special anointing for the woman who is free to seek Him. Her prayer life should explode in miracles!

~Taken from: T.D. Jakes' "Woman Thou Art Loosed!" Bible~

Minister LaVonda Branch will share with you some wisdom on that Proverbs 31 Woman, while Overseer Patience Scott will share from a wife and mother's perspective in the upcoming pages.

A Message for Wives
[Minister LaVonda Branch]

Often times I hear women say they want to be a Proverbs 31 Woman. When we read about her, we realize that this woman had it going on and she was all that! She was definitely about her business. She was a wife, mother and businesswoman who cared about her appearance. Her clothing was fine linen and purple (which represents royalty).

When you know you are a queen, you will begin to dress like one. 1 Peter 2:9 confirms your royalty. Queens dress with dignity and select garments that will adorn their temple. They don't dress any way they please.

Wives, we have to be mindful of how we dress at all times. Proverbs 31 does not mention anything about this woman dressing sexy or provocative. I believe if we saw her today, she would be a classy lady. In 1 Peter 3:4, it tells us that we should clothe ourselves with the beauty that comes from within; the unfading beauty of a gentle and quiet spirit, which is precious to God. Sometimes your husband may adore certain outfits that you wear, however; it still does not mean that you should be "eye candy" for every man. You can wear next to nothing in your bedroom; just make sure that when you leave the house, you are well covered. There are so many ways to be fashionable and yet still represent Christ. You can always spice things up when you step outside by accessorizing with shoes, jewelry, etc. Try some new lipstick, eye shadow, nail polish or hairstyle. Get creative!

Wives, did you know that according to 1 Corinthians 6:19, your body is a temple of the Holy Spirit? Have you ever seen a crazy looking temple? A temple is a place of worship. Your temple (body) houses the Holy Spirit. You should have a desire to worship God even in the way you dress. When you walk out of the door; is God being glorified? Is God getting the glory when you willingly entice other men? Oftentimes, wives will seek attention from other men because their husbands completely ignore them. It is best to put that effort toward pleasing God and your own husband. If your heart is truly committed and you are totally surrendered to God, you would allow the Holy Spirit to help you get dressed in the morning. Romans 12:1 says to present your bodies a living sacrifice, holy, acceptable to God, which is your reasonable service.

How are you presenting your body? Do you look like a harlot or holy when leaving home? Verse 3 tells us not to be conformed to this world, but be transformed by the renewing of your mind. So many women are doing just what the Bible instructs them not to do. I firmly believe when you know better, then you should do better. After reading this book, you can no longer say that no one shared these principles with you. **You are a bride to Christ first, then your husband.**

A Message for Mothers
[Overseer Patience Scott]

I can remember my mother's desire for me to be a ballerina, but my father put a ball in my hand at an early age. That was the end of my tutu and slippers. I later went on to earn a basketball scholarship for the University of Richmond. My father and sideline coach made it very clear that I was to get the job done on the court, but when I came off the court, I was to be a lady. At the end of my senior year in college, my father thanked me for remaining a lady as he was aware of the many pressures, including homosexuality. As I reflect back on that time in my life, I know that it was the prayers and Godly examples of my mother and grandmother that kept me.

My mother prayed that her daughters would be *corner stone polished after the similitude of a palace* according to Psalm 144:12. My mother set the example in our home of what Proverbs 31 depicts. She always presented herself so clean and she was put together. It was rare for her not to receive a compliment about her beauty or the clothes she was wearing when we were out. She always responded; "Praise God!" I used to be so embarrassed as she consistently gave God the praise no matter where we were. Growing up as an athlete, I loved wearing sweat suits because they were comfortable and after all, I would be going to work out at the gym. I can recall my mom asking me most of the time; "Is that what you're wearing?" I had an attitude and would get so upset with her. I resented her for a period of time - the very person that God was using to show me a glimpse of my future and who I could become based on the authenticity that He placed within me.

Having two daughters of my own, ages 4 and 2, I now understand my mother's desire for her girls to look their best at all times. I don't know about you, but it upsets me to see mothers that are well-polished and their children disheveled. However, don't let the dress or someone's charm fool you. Proverbs 31:30 (Message Translation) reads, *"Charm can mislead and beauty soon fades. The woman to be admired and praised is the woman who lives in the Fear-of-God."* Part of living in the fear of God, is understanding that your life is not your own and recognizing the time that God took to uniquely shape you while you were in the womb. Before someone else acknowledges His creation of you; you must praise Him for how He made you. It is then that He will begin to fine tune your taste as it pertains to fashion. The compliments that you receive will be primarily based on your love for Him; expressed through your dress.

Mothers, know that your daughters are watching you. You may not be Ms. Fashionista, but make sure you don't allow their dress to compromise who they are and who God desires for them to become. In addition, know the power of your words. Daughters need affirmation as they mature and develop. If it doesn't come from you, they will dress to attract the attention of others. We must understand that everything we have been given is for a purpose. Someone may never come to church but will notice an outfit or a pair of shoes. Allow those opportunities to share the love of Christ and change someone's destiny. We are the church and our standards should not change because we are away from the sanctuary.

I have been told that I look like my mother and I receive that as a major compliment. Today my mother is my friend, mentor and personal shopper. As a result of her influence and words of affirmation, I am training my polished daughters at an early age to represent God while expressing their uniqueness in all that they do. Although I have matured in my taste for fashion and continuously growing in that area, I still enjoy wearing sweat suits!

Exercise: Take about five minutes each day for a week and look at yourself in the mirror. I mean **REALLY** look at yourself and allow the Lord to show you who you are and how He sees you. Write down your observations of how you see yourself as well as what you hear and begin to work on making the necessary adjustments.

Chapter 7

ARE YOU BLENDING IN OR STANDING OUT?

In one of the previous chapters, I mentioned the phrase; "to thy own self be true." I want to look at that same phrase from a biblical angle. We all know that our old nature died when we were born again.

In Galatians 2:20, it tells us that it is no longer you who live, but Christ who lives in you. Are you living true to your new Christ-nature, or are you denying who you really are by acting as if your old self is still alive?

What messages are we sending out by the way we clothe our bodies? If you are showing a lot of skin to get attention from men, I can assure you that you will attract the wrong type of man. A man may take you out on a date mainly for one reason; to see more of what you tempted him with in the beginning. I can guarantee you that he will never take you home to meet his mother. He is going to take the one that is dressed in a respectable manner. Do you think he will introduce you to his father with your cleavage exposed? I am sure you can answer that question. Please allow this to marinate in your Spirit.

I was talking with a young man in the doctor's office recently who was taking pictures of my eyes. We began to talk about my book and he shared the following:

I am only 25 years of age and occasionally I go to the club. Most of the young females barely have on anything. They leave very little to the imagination. It is almost impossible not to look, but in my mind the question is always; "what happened to her self-respect?" I would never consider taking her home to meet my parents. He indicated that he wishes females could wake up and realize that they don't have to dress like whores to get attention. The conversation between the two of us was **on** after that. He also shared that he was a professional photographer. In his profession, he is in a position to meet women from all backgrounds. He spoke about a woman of integrity.

Regardless of whether you are a teenager or a young female adult waiting on your Boaz, it is difficult in today's society to be an individualist, have a mind of your own and think for yourself. The peer pressure is greater now than ever before. Many teens have lost their identity trying to be a part of the crowd. You were fearfully and wonderfully made. It takes a strong person to stand out, but it takes little to no effort on your part to be a follower. Have you ever thought of being a leader?

Consider creating your own styles and have others wanting to dress like you. Become a trendsetter in a modest/fashionable way. If you start it, I guarantee you that others will follow. Because of your modest dress style, God could give you just what you need to start your own clothing line. We never know the plans He has for our lives. He has already promised you that He would honor your faithfulness. Why not seek Him daily for guidance in the way you should dress? **Dare to be different!**

Have you ever considered starting a Christian Modeling Group? This will surely give you the platform to show others how to dress to represent God. Most teens and young adults enjoy fashion shows. This is a way of allowing your light to shine in a fun way. This is an excellent time to have someone to speak briefly on "Modesty in Dress." You may have a friend who has that special gift of designing clothes. Maybe God has given you the gift of organization; imagine what could happen if the two of you decide to put your gifts and talents together. Make an all out effort to search among your group and bond with those who may have similar goals. He wants to use you for His glory!

When you come to worship, are you dressing in a manner that pleases God? You must ask yourself; am I a Man-Pleaser or a God-Pleaser? If you are a God-Pleaser, why is there so much cleavage exposed? Why are you showing every curve that God has given you? If you see someone in church whose style you admire, why not suggest that the two of you go shopping together. I am sure that you both will gain from the experience. God has great plans for you (Jeremiah 29:11), but He must prepare you in advance. That definitely includes your dress attire. You want others to be able to see Christ in you.

In Nancy Leigh DeMoss article; "Mirror, Mirror on the wall: The Decision to Live Your Life For God's Glory," she states the following:

"Your clothing should be tight enough to show that you're a woman, but loose enough to show that you're a lady!"

Remember that it is possible to have a modest outward appearance while having the heart of a Pharisee (critical, self-righteous and judgmental towards those who don't see things the way you do). Modesty doesn't mean that you have the corner on truth. Give God room and time to work in the lives of other people. Don't say; "Because I see it that way, that's how it should be." Remember you are not the Holy Spirit.

The Blessings of Modesty

Modesty is something good, desirable and precious. There are many blessings you can experience as a result of modesty. They include:

Peace: You'll know that you are obedient to God.

Power: You'll be free from enslavement to fashion, fads and others' opinions.

Protection: You'll be guarded from the wrong kind of attention from the wrong kind of men. (Dressing modestly doesn't guarantee that "the wrong kind of men" will never give you unwanted attention, but it sure helps)!

Privilege: You'll experience greater freedom in marriage as your body is reserved only for your husband.

Praise: You'll be valued for spiritual and heart qualities more than physical characteristics.

Copyright Revive Our Hearts: Taken from Nancy Leigh DeMoss booklet, "The Look: Does God really care what I wear?" Used with permission. www.ReviveOurHearts.com.

On the next page is the Dress Code for Henrico Juvenile and Domestic Relations Court for the County of Henrico. In checking with the other jurisdictions, the dress codes are the same. As you notice, you are not able to appear before the judge dressed inappropriately. The purpose of this dress code is to encourage order during and respect for the proceedings in the courtroom.

Should the dress code be any different for the House of God? Some judges don't even believe in God. So why is there more respect for the judge who is in charge in his courtroom and less respect for the Man or Woman of God who is responsible for feeding your soul in the House of God?

As we are directed to come to order when we enter the courtroom in our appropriate dress, why don't we have a greater respect for coming into the House of God in our proper attire to worship the King of Kings and Lord of Lords? He deserves our very best!

Dress Code
Virginia:

In the Henrico Juvenile and Domestic Relations District Court for the County of Henrico

It is hereby ORDERED that all parties involved in matters before the Juvenile and Domestic Relations District Court of Henrico County dress in a respectful and appropriate manner, indicative of the dignity of court proceedings when entering the court building. This includes but is not limited, to the following guidelines:

1. Midriffs/stomachs are to be covered at all times.
2. No halter-tops, tank tops, or muscle shirts are to be worn. Backs are to be covered at all times.
3. No miniskirts or short-shorts allowed.
4. With religious and medical exception, no hats, headscarves, headbands, or kerchiefs may be worn.
5. Shoes must be worn at all times.
6. No exposed underwear.
7. No clothing with obscene or vulgar wording or pictures.
8. Trousers are to be worn at the waistline and shirttails are to be tucked in.

This dress code is designed to encourage order during and respect for the proceedings in the Juvenile and Domestic Relations District Court. The Court expects and appreciates the full cooperation of the public and all employees with the terms of this Order. Violation of this Order may result in a finding of contempt.

In this chapter there are several testimonies from young ladies who are living the life of holiness. They are living examples of how you can do it with style, class and poise. They were selected because of their "spirits of consistency." Whenever you see them, regardless of whether it is the first or fourth Sunday, you can tell that thought went into what they were going to wear. They are very stylish in their dress and are determined that they are not going to compromise. They are excited about representing God in every area of their lives – especially their dress. They are sharing because they sincerely care about you. Their main desire is that you will profit by their mistakes or lack of mistakes.

Throughout this book and in the testimonies to follow, the writers are referring to some of the same scriptures. This is no coincidence. I encourage you to read, study and meditate on those scriptures. In doing so, your mindsets will be renewed by the Word of God.

The Style of a Fashionable Christian
[Testimony of Shamece Stewart]

Who would have thought that I would be writing about the style of a fashionable Christian? I did not feel that I was qualified to do so, but for the grace of God. Style for me is an expression of the heart. When you purchase different items of clothing, there is an ideal look you desire to achieve. Where does this ideal look come from? Could it be a confidence in who you are, or a lack thereof? If the latter is true, one tries to make up through dressing inappropriately.

During my teenage years, I thought the more you showed the better you look. I was out there in the world and I lived for the approval of men and the attention and comments that came with the skimpy dress. The media gives one the image that flesh is attractive and that's how you get attention. The statement is true, but what they don't express is the type of attention you are attracting.

Now I understand that my body is a palace for my King and my King alone. I don't dress the same. The King I am referring to is not a human but the King of Kings and Lord of Lords. God placed in my heart the way He viewed me by writing 1 Peter 2:9 which states: **"But ye are a chosen generation, a royal priesthood, an holy nation, a peculiar people; that ye should show forth the praises of him who hath called you out of darkness into his marvelous light."** As you read those words, what comes to mind? You began to understand that you are valuable.

As God loved on me, He spoke to my heart about who I was to Him and the plans He had for me. Now that I am saved and my mindset has changed, there is no longer a desire to reveal what God desires to be hidden. If you are a child of God, what you wear on a daily basis should represent Him. You never know who may be watching! But remember, God is always watching!

Modesty is The Best Policy
[Testimony of Sheree Hilliard]

Over the years I have begun to understand the value of appearance and being aware of how a woman of God should dress when representing Christ our King. While inner beauty is very important, it is exciting to know that we can honor and bring our Father glory in our outward appearance as well. On many occasions, I have given thought to what it means to reverence God by the way I dress, and how the daughter of a King should dress. But this wasn't always the case for me.

When I was younger, I struggled with low self-esteem that lasted into my adult years. As a result, there was always a battle in me to dress modestly while growing up. I always strived to dress in that manner, but from time to time in my struggle, I would select a "not so modest" outfit because I wanted to be complimented and noticed by guys. I did not believe that I was beautiful. I knew that I had a nice shape so I wanted to show it off. I was seeking attention and needing to fill a void. But the Lord worked on me and helped me realize my self-worth and those things that did not line up with what He thought about me. Now in my adulthood, I understand that I am fearfully and wonderfully made. God said so and I don't need anyone to validate that.

Along my journey I found myself choosing tight fitting jeans that would show off my behind. I also had a love for tops that exposed my back. I remember at a young age buying and wearing an outfit that showed my stomach with short shorts because I was trying to be cute. I remember a specific instance in my teenage years where I picked a dress that was very short to wear because I knew there would be a guy that I liked at the place where I was going. I wanted him to notice me. I would wear certain clothes when I wanted the attention because of something deep on the inside of me that needed to be corrected.

In high school, I participated on a modeling team that did fashion shows on a regular basis. Some of the scenes included modeling swimsuits and lingerie. I remember battling with what to wear during those times and struggling between modesty and my flesh. I would try to pick something that was as modest as you could get for the scene. I would justify what I wore by telling myself; compared to what the others were wearing, mine wasn't that bad. But I still participated and modeled in those scenes because the attention and recognition felt good. I remember my Pastor at the time coming to one of the fashion shows. I didn't know he was there and he did not expect to see what he saw. Later on he spoke with me and expressed his disappointment because I was one of the youth who was supposed to be setting an example in my ministry. My heart felt heavy and I never forgot that conversation. I continued to participate because I was young and having fun.

Later on down the road, I had my first experience at a "Go-Go" club. My motive was again to have fun, turn heads and show off the figure that I had. I remember wearing a skirt that had high splits on both sides (because that was the style at the time) and a shear layer on top running from about the hip down.

Basically, you could see through my skirt with only the top of it being covered. I felt somewhat uncomfortable and got the attention that I was seeking, but this time it didn't feel good. I had to deal with a guy in the club that whole night who tried to take me home based on what he saw. It was not a good experience at all.

After that night, I took a look at myself and realized that something wasn't right in me and that I needed a change. I thank God for the process of deliverance in this area. I had to get in His Word and understand the truth. Psalm 139 is where I began to find my comfort and deliverance. When God began to heal the inside of me, it was as if something that had me bound for years had lost its grip. I am finally free! It was a process. Until the change came on the inside of me, the outside could not begin to line up. My healing started on the inside and then the Lord dealt with the outside so that He could use it for His glory.

Here are some things that I have learned along the way. In regards to our wardrobe, if we remember that we are God's representatives here on earth, then this area of our life should reflect what we believe. Take a moment to think about the role of an Ambassador. As an ambassador, your job is to portray the place that you are representing in a positive light. The Bible says in 2 Corinthians that we are Ambassadors of Christ and that God is making His appeal through us (John 15:19). Therefore, if we represent Christ who is in Heaven, and He tells us that we are in the world but not of the world, then we should look the part. Ask yourself, if you were standing before the Lord, would you be able to wear what you have on and be comfortable? Would your wardrobe reverence Him? The role of an ambassador is to confidently represent the place they are from in excellence for a specific purpose. Therefore, if lust and sex sells in the world; we are called to do the opposite. As women of God, we should be examples of holiness in our attire. The Word says that our bodies are temples (1 Corinthians 6:19). Just as your work should be unto the Lord, so should your dress be unto the Lord.

As a lady it can be challenging to dress as I call it; "cute but covered" because of the style of clothes that are sold in today's society. They are not always the most appropriate and at times it takes extra effort, but it can be done. You can be stylish, trendy and modest without being "old fashioned" as some would say. The beauty about being excellent in your appearance is that you will never go wrong with being modestly dressed for whatever the occasion. It's a matter of finding what works best for you and embracing the style which God has placed on the inside of you. It is something that even if you don't have a lot of money, you can do your best on the level where you are. You don't have to spend a lot or even dress like someone else. You are the designer's original and there is only one YOU. Be yourself and develop your own beauty regimen. Remember that being classy never goes out of style.

A great example can be found in Esther where the Bible speaks about Queen Esther and the other women who were to be presented to the King. They all had to go through a specific beauty regimen (Esther Chapter 2). They were not allowed to approach the King without putting forth their best in appearance. I personally believe that none of them were used to this kind of treatment and it was a process and transformation for them. As we go through the process of being molded into His image while we are learning, you may have to ask from time to time if your attire is appropriate. When in doubt, ask someone you trust to tell you the truth. Remember that you are still in the learning process; no one has arrived. With time and practice, there should be a visible difference until it flows naturally. Your example should be consistent across the board. If you are modest around certain people and revealing around others, then check your motives. Another thing to keep in mind is the Bible also says that we should not want to cause our brothers to stumble. As women, we have the ability to dress in a manner that causes a man to lust or a young lady to think that certain inappropriate attire is acceptable. You should not be a distraction in either situation by the way you are dressed; (a true man of God can discern a true woman of God). Respect yourself and what you are carrying!

As sisters, mothers, daughters, role models, friends, etc., we can raise the standard and be that example of how to dress with excellence. Just as honesty is the best policy, modesty is the best policy. People see you before you open your mouth. A woman's appearance speaks volumes everywhere she goes. Again, we have to recognize what we are carrying and who we are representing. The bottom line; people are watching for the God in you to see if they should serve him too. Could you represent the Kingdom of God at its finest with your wardrobe? Dress your best to reverence God. He deserves it!

"FASHIONABLY MODEST"
[Testimony of Minister Damilola Adeoye]

How should a woman of God dress in order to glorify God and not conform to the world's style of dress?

I thank God for the opportunity to discuss how to represent Him through our dress. As a woman of God, the way I dress is a reflection of God and my parents. Growing up as the only girl with three brothers within a Christian Nigerian family, we had our own tailors that customized our attire. Our mom always had us well-dressed so that everywhere we went, everyone knew we were Captain Adeoye's kids and most importantly, we represented God. My father always taught me that no matter what I do or where I am, I should always know God is watching me in everything I do. This is still my conviction today.

I am a member of Bloodline, a neo-soul gospel singing group. I am always mindful of how I dress and carry myself, not only in church settings but also outside of church on a daily basis. I always prepare my outfit the day before church with the guidance of the Holy Spirit. Then when I have it together, I put it on and stand before the mirror and make sure no cleavage is showing. Whether I am wearing pants, a skirt, or a dress, I make sure they are not too tight or revealing. You shouldn't have your "goodies" on display. I'll raise my hands so I can be "sure." I live by the motto; "When in doubt, throw it out." If you have to ask whether it's okay to wear, then the rule of thumb is; you probably shouldn't. You should always make sure you carry at least one or two safety pins for last minute adjustments or emergencies.

If you want everyone to be able to receive your ministry in song, your dress shouldn't distract people. In the gospel industry, we have a lot of anointed singers but their outfits give us a totally different message from what their music is saying. Just because you're covered, isn't enough. If it's tight and you can draw the silhouette of your shape in your outfit, that's a problem. Seeing cleavage and behinds don't lead people into worship. We have to be mindful that our dress could be a stumbling block for our brothers in Christ. There are men trying to live for God and do the right thing. We don't want them to fall into lust, even if it's just in their mind. Our attire should not add to their struggles. I want them to be able to see us as their sisters representing God.

Be cautious of your body when you gain or lose weight; your clothes will fit differently. The cliché in fashion is; size 8 is the new size 6, therefore they feel that tighter is sexier. That's the world's mindset. As women of God we can't allow that mindset to govern our wardrobes. If you are blessed in the chest, make sure you are well supported and fully covered. If you are blessed with a behind, you need to keep it covered but not tight. We don't want to see or know your secrets or that you're wearing Victoria Secrets either. The length of your dress or skirt is very important, I take that seriously. I think dresses that are a little bit below the knees are appropriate. If you have to wear high heels, a 5-inch or lower, it will make the dress or skirt appear even shorter. God help you if you choose to sit down.

And to all my sisters who have been sitting under the Word and have been taught on how to dress, you are accountable for your actions if you don't make adjustments to your wardrobe. It's not just about you and what looks good on you. Young women are watching us and we have to set a good example so they can follow in our footsteps and dress "creatively modest." We are representing the Kingdom and don't have to conform by acting or dressing like the world. We can create our own styles without adapting to the world's style. Every outfit doesn't look great on everyone just because two people wear the same size. God created us individually and in a unique way. We are fearfully and wonderfully made. So find out what works for your body type. Enhance it in a godly fashion that will make God pleased with you. All I want to do is please my Heavenly Father and do that by carrying myself as His daughter.

I am honored and humbled to have been asked to share my knowledge and views on representing God through my dress. I pray that everyone who reads this will benefit from the information I shared.

About The Author

Shirley R. Hawkins is a native of Richmond, Virginia. She received her education from the Richmond Public Schools and attended Virginia Commonwealth University.

She retired from the Commonwealth of Virginia (Virginia Industries for the Blind) as Supervisor in 1995 after 32 years of service.

She is the mother of one daughter, Minister LaVonda Branch and one granddaughter, Kyia Hobson, a student at Liberty University in Lynchburg, Virginia.

Shirley's mentoring Spirit caught fire when she was in her teen years. She has never wavered from this special call on her life. Shirley has mentored many young people, and because of her capacity to mentor, her vision for a modeling/production company for teens was born in 2002. While recognizing the special leadership and organizational abilities of her granddaughter Kyia, she christened it, "Kyia's Productions." This 14-week curriculum taught teens the following: Basic & Advanced Modeling Techniques, Health & Fitness, Skin Care & Makeup, Grooming & Personal Hygiene, Social Skills, Hair Care and Personal Development & Wardrobe Styling.

She has also served as executive producer of the annual fundraiser; an "Evening of Elegance" which included a fashion show, dinner and various gospel artists.

Now at the seasoned age of 68, and a decade later, she has penned her first book. This book is a challenge to women of all ages to dress in a manner so that God can get the honor, glory and praise! Known as a classy lady and for her great sense of style, Shirley would like to share with women the importance of being fashionable and modest at the same time.

As a passionate follower of Jesus Christ, Shirley is a member of Mt. Gilead Full Gospel International Ministries, Richmond, Virginia under the dynamic leadership of Bishop Daniel Robertson Jr. and Co-Pastor Elena Robertson. She serves on the Intercessory Prayer Ministry. Many young people at Mt. Gilead fondly refer to her as ("G-Ma") for Grandma.

***I Can Do All Things Through Christ
Who Strengthens Me"***
Philippians 4:13

Notes

Notes

Notes

Thank you for purchasing

**Mirror On The Wall:
Would My Dress Cause
My Brother To Fall?**

It is my prayer that you received
revelation and you will share
this information with others.

**TO ORDER ADDITIONAL COPIES
OR CONTACT US:**

Website: www.srhministries.com
Email Address: srhministries@gmail.com
Phone: (804) 754-8658
or
Mailing Address

**Shirley R. Hawkins
Shirley R. Hawkins Ministries
P. O. Box 29165
Richmond, VA 23242**